Franco's Mass Graves
Breaking the Silence in Spain

Emilio Silva Barrera

Franco's Mass Graves

Breaking the Silence in Spain

Translated by

VERONICA DEAN-THACKER
Transylvania University

and

SHELBY G. THACKER
Asbury University

Juan de la Cuesta
Newark, Delaware

Juan de la Cuesta Hispanic Monographs
An imprint of Linguatext, LLC.
Newark, Delaware 19711 USA
(302) 453-8695

www.JuandelaCuesta.com

MANUFACTURED IN THE UNITED STATES OF AMERICA
*

ISBN: 978-1-58871-403-9 (HB)
ISBN: 978-1-58871-404-6 (PB)

Table of Contents

Translators' Note

THIS BOOK WAS FIRST published in 2003, and we have used for our translation the 2006 edition from Temas de Hoy, which includes the prologue by Isaías Lafuente. The book should have been translated into English twenty years ago, as so much has happened in the interim with regard to the discovery of mass graves in Spain and political action involving the Association for the Recovery of Historical Memory, both of which are not included in this translation.

In order to avoid confusion with the term *republicano* (the political left or supporters of same), we are leaving the term in Spanish and in italics. Additionally, the term *desaparecido* (a person who was intentionally "disappeared" by the opposition), will be left in italics or translated into English as "disappeared" in quotation marks.

Biography

EMILIO SILVA BARRERA was born in the town of Elizondo, in the province of Navarra, in 1965. As a child, he spent his summers in Pereje, a small town in the Bierzo region of northwestern Spain, the birthplace of his grandfather, Emilio Silva Faba, who was murdered in October of 1936 for being a member of *Izquierda Republicana* (the political left).

Since graduating from the University of Madrid with a major in Sociology, Silva has dedicated his professional life to Journalism. In March of 2000, he discovered the place which held the remains of his grandfather and twelve other men. Seven months later, with the help of archaeologists, medical examiners and other volunteers, he exhumed the remains of those who would be known as the Priaranza Thirteen. As a result of that exhumation, and with the collaboration of Santiago Macías, he founded the Association for the Recovery of Historical Memory, of which he is president. He balances his professional life with helping the hundreds of families who have contacted the Association to find their "disappeared" relatives.

To my mother, FE (FAITH); her memory walks with me.

To my father, EMILIO SILVA SANTÍN,
because this is also his story.

To PALMA, NICOLÁS, CLAUDIA and JULIA.

To SANTIAGO MACÍAS,
for the road we are sharing.

Acknowledgments

To Julia, Rosi, Marifé, Cristina y Nazareth, Ramón Silva, Manuel Silva, Javier Ceballo, Juan Antonio Palacios, Jesús Alpuente, José Emilio Cobertera, Santiago Macías, Susana Álvarez, María Encina Prada, Julio Vidal, Mari Luz González, Lourdes Herrasti, Remedios Prada, Venancio Carlón, Francisco Etxeberria, Aníbal Arroyo, Teresa Rivas, Francisco Ferrándiz, Theo Francos, Daniel Fernández, José Luis Ramón, Elena Reviriego, Javier Ortiz, Jimi Jiménez, Esther de Ferrol, Javier Rodrigo, José María Rojas, José Ignacio Casado, Sociedad de Ciencias Aranzadi, voluntarios del Servicio Civil Internacional, Isabel González, Alejandro Álvarez, Vicente Moreira, Asunción Álvarez, Carlos Agüero, Belén Guerra, Ariel Jerez, José Masa, Juan Manuel Llorca, María Álvarez, Ventureta Ballus, Montserrat Sans, Asunción Esteban, Javier Castán, Olga Frutos, Maider Telletxea, Asier Olazábal, Jesús Tapia, Benja Arregui, Jorge López, Eloy Alonso, Sofía Moro, Rafael López, Paqui de Sevilla, Ángel del Río, Cecilio Lafuente, Carlos Elordi, Fernando Berlín, Iñaki Gabilondo, Isadora Guardia, Julio Llamazares, Mary Maccoy, María José Andrade, Thomas Kreutzmann, Xosé Lois Carrión, Fernando Magán, Manuel Perona, Nuria Gallach, Miguel Sánchez Tostado, Pablo Sánchez León, Paloma Aguilar, Javier Rodríguez Alarcón, Olga Pérez, Ana Vanegas, Ángel Fuentes, Carlos Slepoy, Carlos Castresana, Sanjuana Martínez, Carlos Iriart, Ben Donahue, Maite Gómez, Óscar Carlón, Luis Doyague, Jesús Montero, Óscar Gutiérrez, Rosa Regàs, Ana Pérez, Pedro Peinado, Fernando Antón, La Gavilla Verde, Jóvenes del Jerte, Asociación de Amigos de las Brigadas Internacionales, Asociación Pozos del Caudé, Asociación Memoria Histórica y Justicia de Andalucía, Asociaciones para la Recuperación de la Memoria Histórica de: Cataluña, Extremadura, Asturias, Galicia, Jaén, Málaga, ... And all those individuals and groups who work to dignify the memory of the *republicanos*, both men and women, who formed our first democracy.

Poem by the Author

To all the *republicanos* and *republicanas* (men and women on the political Left) who are still afraid to speak after so many years of democracy.

Es un silencio largo, cruel, pesado,
es una soledad que arrasa el cielo,
es un lugar distante, un desconsuelo,
es un miedo brutal, antepasado.

It is a long, cruel, heavy silence,
a solitude that obliterates the heavens,
a distant place, an affliction,
a brutal, ancestral fear.

Es una voz inmóvil, roca y hielo,
es un sonido sordo, plomo alado,
es angustia, es dolor petreficado,
es una mano inerte a ras del suelo.

It is an unmoving voice, hard and frozen,
a hollow sound, a leaden weight,
anguish, petrified sorrow,
a lifeless hand along the ground.

Su boca no funciona como boca,
hay memoria en su voz enmudecida,
que espanta siempre al verbo que la toca.

His mouth does not act like a mouth,
there is memory in his silenced voice,
startled at any sound it hears.

Su labio, más que labio es una herida,
un trágico pasado que disloca,
la amarga comisura de su vida.

His lip, more than lip, is a wound,
a tragic past that twists his life
like the bitter corners of his mouth.

Emilio Silva Barrera

Prologue by the Author

ON THE 19TH OF November 1933, Spain held its first democratic elections with universal suffrage, the first time Spanish women were allowed to vote. This unprecedented event occurred during the Second Republic, 1931-1939. (Spain had ceased being a constitutional monarchy after general elections in February, 1931.) The outcome of the 1933 elections resulted in a peaceful change of administration, and in those first years of the Republic Spain began to make a concerted effort to modernize, building thousands of schools, instituting the separation of Church and State, decriminalizing homosexuality, legislating divorce and guaranteeing women's rights.

On February 12, 1936, general elections were held again, with the outcome showing a win for the leftist coalition known as the Popular Front. When the new President of the Government was elected on May 8, 1936, it was without incident. However, on July 18th of that year, a group of military officers staged a coup d'état to seize power by force. When the majority of Spaniards refused to support the coup, the officers started a war, achieving their objectives three years later.

Throughout the three-year civil war, the military insurgents received the help of thousands of soldiers from the armies of Adolf Hitler and Benito Mussolini. In the end, they defeated the democratically elected government and instituted a cruel dictatorship. That marked the first victory for fascism in Europe and, one might say, the beginning of World War II.

For nearly forty years, the dictator Francisco Franco refused to hold democratic elections, and he relentlessly persecuted his political and moral opponents. Between 1939 and 1945, more than 55,000 people were murdered. Half a million were forced to go into exile at the war's end simply to save their lives, and the majority of those died without being able to return to their hometowns. Three hundred concentration camps were built, including one on the island of Formentera (Canary Islands) exclusively for homosexuals. Women suffered a huge setback and endured official campaigns promoting the idea that their purpose in life was to serve their husbands. In 1954, Spain began purchasing the Polio vaccine, but only those who had fought for the fascist military victory had access to it; all others were left exposed to the virus. The economic and political corruption of the Franco regime left his family with an enormous fortune, and the wealth of some of Spain's major corporations today was generated early on by the use of political slaves.

Prior to his death, the dictator had designated as his successor Juan Carlos de Borbón, grandson of Spain's previous king, Alfonso XIII. Franco died on November 20, 1975, and the political elite commenced orchestrating a return to democracy. Their primary goal was not to be judged for any of their crimes. Additionally, they determined to conceal from the new generations of Spaniards the atrocities they committed in order to maintain power and prevent, for forty years, the contamination of their institutions by non-conservative ideas.

On June 15, 1977, new democratic elections were held for Parliament. The pro-Republic parties had not been legalized, because the Francoist elites wanted to prevent any monarchy vs. republic debate or any discussion of the criminals of the dictatorship being subjected to the justice system. Therefore, the first item that the new Parliament approved was a Law of Amnesty, which effectively exonerated those guilty of crimes associated with the dictatorship.

In spite of the attempt by Spanish institutions to bury the past, exhumations of common graves were carried out in some towns and villages. Without archaeologists, without medical examiners, with only the love of close relatives and friends, and a pick and shovel, the families retrieved the bones and took them to the cemeteries. All of that momentum came to a halt on February 23, 1981, when a group of military officers held hostage, for nineteen hours, the members of the House of Representatives in Madrid. The same nation that, during the 1936 attempted coup, had marched out to the streets to defend democracy, remained that night in 1981 perfectly still and terrified. What had changed in that society to create this striking difference in reaction? The forty years of the dictatorship's violence and repression had injected a deep fear into those who had spent decades waiting in silence for the return of democracy.

More than twenty years of political silence would have to pass before, in a small town of northwestern Spain, the grandson of a pro-Republic civilian who was murdered by Falangist gunmen at the outset of the civil war would find the unmarked grave containing the remains of his grandfather, together with those of twelve other men, and for the first time a mass grave of victims of Franco would be exhumed scientifically.

That grandson, who managed to have his grandfather identified genetically and reburied next to his grandmother, is the author of these pages. His quest was strictly family-related, but when members of other families who had suffered similar losses approached the open grave during the exhumation, everything changed. In that roadside ditch, in the town of Priaranza del Bierzo, during that first encounter with people whose relatives had remained unaccounted for, the Association for the Recovery of Historical Memory was founded. Almost immediately the ARMH (Asociación para la Recuperación de la Memoria Histórica) began to demand of Spain's institutions an end to impunity, the search for the "disappeared," the teaching of historical truths in schools, and reparations for the families of victims.

This book was written initially in the year 2003 when the ARMH had scientifically exhumed the first mass graves and our society was beginning to see the terrible violations of human rights committed under the dictatorship. The mass graves were a mirror. For decades, public institutions remained silent. Neither the House of Representatives nor the Senate had held a single debate to try to search for the more than 100,000 missing or "disappeared" civilians.

It was the generation of the grandchildren of the victims who began to break the pacts of silence made after the death of the dictator. They complained of having inherited a country full of unmarked graves containing the bodies of thousands of "disappeared" persons, full of monuments to the dictatorship, full of streets with the names of those responsible for unspeakable crimes, a country that mass-produced ignorance of the past and for whose sake it was essential to prevent textbooks from mentioning the crimes of Francoism, something that has changed little even today.

Many things have occurred since that first scientific exhumation. Two laws concerning historical memory have been passed, which have not succeeded in guaranteeing the rights of victims of the dictatorship. Franco's body has been removed from an enormous mausoleum in the basilica built by political slaves, but it has been transferred to a public cemetery, which his victims continue to pay for with their taxes. In Madrid, a few hundred yards from the official seat of the Spanish Government, there is an arch that commemorates the victory of Franco, Hitler and Mussolini, thereby celebrating the murder of the "disappeared" and all the crimes of the dictatorship.

This book was written to tell the story of the birth of a social movement, one whose clear objective was to end the silence imposed on Spain during the transition to democracy in the late 1970's, a silence that benefited the executioners while further harming the victims.

It tells the story of Emilio Silva Faba, the first "disappeared" person from the dictatorship identified through DNA testing, a man from the small town of Pereje in northwestern Spain through which the Road to Santiago passes. Between 1915 and 1925, he lived in Argentina and the United States. He returned to Spain, and when the Republic was established in 1931, he dreamed of a country without illiteracy, with rights and freedoms, where the state institutions would no longer ignore millions of people who could not exercise their rights as citizens.

It also tells the story of a grandson who, while gathering evidence and documentation to write a novel, found the ditch where the body of his grandfather had been buried for sixty-four years, and he decided to change the ending of the book. It tells how sometimes social change can spring up in small places. It explains how memory is a powerful tool that can shed light on what Power wants to conceal. It explains how in discussions about the traumatic past, political, academic, and cultural debates form part of a collective reflection to illuminate the meaning of the past. It shows how when a society looks in the mirror made of earth and bones, it is changing its own identity. And, finally, it recounts how there are people in the world who are ready to fight without ceasing for human dignity, which is perhaps what gives most meaning to our existence.

EMILIO SILVA BARRERA
Madrid 19 September 2023

Prologue by Isaías Lafuente

The time has come for a reckoning.

Can a nation truly allow thousands of its citizens slaughtered like animals by a dictatorial regime to remain buried in roadside ditches? Can it tolerate this behavior while the person responsible for the killings rests under the main altar of a Catholic basilica? The answer is so evident that the question borders on the offensive. But what truly offends the memory of those who were massacred, as well as their wives and husbands, children and grandchildren, is the fact that it can be asked today, six decades later. Only the executioners or those who share the same ideology could respond affirmatively and without any hesitation. But among the rest, there are many people of good will who, because they are unaware or because of the passage of time, are of the opinion that things should be left as they are, undisturbed, without reopening old, seemingly scarred wounds, people who think time will heal the pain, that what is forgotten is healed.

With no hope at all of moving the conscience of members of the first group (Franco sympathizers) even one iota, this book certainly will cause those of the second group to understand that there is no reason to legitimize a society that asks the victims or their descendants to forget, to keep the mass graves closed, so that the filthy laundry of our history does not get aired.

This book is both moving and harsh; it elicits responses that are equally emotional and indignant. It will not leave the reader cold because of one fundamental reason: what is told herein, though it may seem unreal, is true.

Emilio Silva Barrera tells the story of Emilio Silva Faba, his grandfather, and thirteen other men who were murdered on October 16,

1936, at the edge of Priaranza del Bierzo in northwestern Spain by a group of bloodthirsty, fanatical members of the right-wing Falange movement. There was no arrest, no trial, no opportunity to say good-bye. Their bodies were buried in a mass grave that was dug at a cross-roads, a grave that was only opened sixty-four years later when, first fate, and then determination, caused the grandson to exhume the remains.

With the exhumation of his grandfather's body, with the reparation of the debt that history owed his grandmother Modesta, who never was able to give her murdered husband a decent burial, Silva understood very quickly how that day he had not come face-to-face with his own history but with History—that of a generation scarred by a regime that considered anyone with an opposing viewpoint an enemy, and which believed that the best enemy was a dead one. In his grandfather's tomb were twelve other grandfathers, and they were just the first of a long line of grandfathers and grandmothers buried in common graves dug in ditches strewn throughout the length and breadth of the country, covered by lime or by garbage to erase any trace of them, blurred by the earth and by time; graves that once and for all had to be opened.

The Association for the Recovery of Historical Memory was created expressly for this purpose, and this book chronicles the process of converting an individual objective into a collective action, an organization that continues to grow and that, in record time, has gone from the tiny courthouse of rural Villablino (NW Spain) to the United Nations, from the local *Crónica de León* to the *New York Times*, from the remote Bierzo county council to the seat of the central government of Spain in Madrid.

Emilio Silva has stated that, in order to try to sense the anguish, the impotence and the panic of those victims as they were being led to certain death, he often tried to imagine himself in their place. The pages of this book allow the reader to approach that raw experience for himself or herself, to sense what those men and those women must have felt. They also help us to perceive the tremendous fear that tortured the family members who managed to stay alive, a fear sustained and nourished by the dictatorship, but which still held them in its grip at the dawn of democracy, causing them to continue living their drama in silent shame.

Emilio Silva's text reverses the perception that we have of our history, i.e., that our war belongs to the old people—understandably, because of those who remember it firsthand and because of those who reminisce about what they heard from, or what happened to, grandparents and great-grandparents. However, books like this one take us close to a history in which the victims are young people, often adolescents and children, living a full and normal life. Emilio's grandfather was forty-two when he was killed, and he had six children, the youngest only three months old. On the other hand, those who witnessed these killings, the kind of children we see in these pages riding their bikes and wearing shorts, like children anywhere, are now the elderly on the home stretch of their lives.

Discovering the mass murders of those young men and women gives us a good vantage point from which to contemplate the magnitude of the barbarity wreaked on a significant portion of a generation of Spaniards. Seeing those children who witnessed the madness now as elderly convinces us of the brief time that remains to ask them questions and to get their testimony concerning a historical injustice.

As with everything related to the Spanish Civil War, the numbers are never definitive—yet another item that continues to astound at this stage in our history. It has been said that 30,000 unidentified Spaniards could be dead and buried in common graves. And if there are fewer, what difference does it make? Baltasar Garzón[1] pursued Augusto Pinochet because of 1,200 unsolved cases of the "disappeared" in Chile. Then, public opinion in Spain intensified with the possibility of bringing the Chilean dictator to trial. We are not seeing similar enthusiasm in the case of our own "disappeared."

After several decades of living with terrorism and with the world that protects it through its silence, we have arrived at the conclusion that there are silences that not only protect the status quo but, in the process, also create accomplices. If Memory is not stirred definitively and widely, if we do not learn the truth, identify the victims and pay

---

1   A Spanish judge and key figure in securing the extradition of Chilean president Augusto Pinochet to Spain on human rights abuse charges.

them posthumous respect—first and foremost, a decent burial—, then that captive and disarmed Memory will allow the nationalist cause to have attained its final objective.

Fortunately, there are books such as the one you are holding that will prevent this from happening. I have the feeling that the road taken by the author is unstoppable. Some day when this black page of our history has turned appropriately for all, we will have to reread it to remember how it all started: that morning in October, 60 years after that crime when the grandson opened the shameful mass grave of his grandfather Emilio and twelve other men, unearthed at a crossroad in Priaranza del Bierzo under a walnut tree.

Of course, then, in no town in this country, when someone asks about those killed in the civil war, will anyone be able to reply: "In this town there are more dead outside the cemetery than inside it."

Toward Righting a Wrong

1
Awakening Memory

"I̦N THIS TOWN THERE are more dead outside the cemetery than inside it." The old man had protected his eyes from the sun with his hand above his forehead and looked at me from head to toe before responding to the question that I had asked him, i.e., whether he knew if there were mass graves from the Civil War in that town. He stood there staring at me, waiting for some additional reaction. I thanked him and walked on, convinced that he had exaggerated, perhaps trying to impress me. I continued in search of other possible witnesses without being completely aware that I was about to discover that that man who was around 80 years old and who walked with a shuffle had limited himself to a harsh reality about which until then I was unaware. Neither he nor I knew that my life and the lives of many families were going to change in a drastic way from that precise instant.

It was Sunday, March 5, 2000. Spain was wrapped up in the final stages of its general elections which one week later would yield as the winner the Partido Popular.[2] I had traveled to Bierzo in search of documentation for a report. I wanted to contact older people who had lived through the war and the aftermath in the area around Pereje, the hometown of my father's family, in which my grandmother had to take refuge with her six children after her husband was murdered.

That morning I left Madrid very early, and upon arriving in Ponferrada I went to the home of Arsenio Marcos, an old friend of my father who, whenever he saw me (from one vacation to the next), would

---

2 The Partido Popular, or People's Party, is Spain's main Conservative Party.

share with me some comment or other about my grandfather. Arsenio, a militant communist, spent several years in prison after a comrade "gave up" a list of names during an extremely harsh interrogation. When he was set free, he struggled to recover the job he had had prior to his incarceration. And now, given our democracy, he was able to recover all of his rights, including his years of service.

I had called Arsenio from Madrid to ask for his help. He contacted several neighbors in the area who were willing to talk with me about their experiences during the Civil War and the postwar period. My interest was centered specifically on the people who had to flee and leave everything behind in a mad rush.

We spent that Sunday morning talking in the village of Cabañas Raras with a friend who had done his compulsory military service with Arsenio. He told us that sometimes people who were fleeing would stop at his house, and that they had a dog that possessed a singular quality during the most difficult years of the postwar period: it only barked when those who were approaching were members of the Civil Guard.[3] (His story did not lack accounts of escapees, and of the network of homes in which they were certain to find refuge, from the Bierzo to Orense, to avoid having to sleep outdoors.) Afterwards, I took Arsenio to Ponferrada where he invited me to have lunch in his home. During the chat after the meal, he began talking about my grandfather, and at one point he alluded to the place in which his body had been left buried in a common grave next to those of twelve other men. He also told me how they had been murdered and who could have been responsible for his death.

The war dead had always been present in my family, more for the silence which surrounded their names than stories about them. The body of my grandfather had never been found. My grandmother tried to get help from the political and religious authorities, but she never heard back from any of them. Arsenio had several clues about where the grave could be found. He talked to me about a town close to Ponferrada along the old highway to Orense. The man with whom we had arranged to meet in the afternoon called to say that a family issue had

---

3   The Spanish *Guardia Civil* or Civil Guard, a paramilitary police force loyal to the Franco cause.

arisen and that he would be unable to meet with us. That little incident altered the direction of my visit and resulted in an unexpected change in my life. We spent the rest of the afternoon trying to locate the burial site of my grandfather.

Arsenio thought the grave was in Villalibre de la Jurisdicción,[4] a town that, as they say in those parts, is ironically neither free nor has any jurisdiction. We crossed a bridge over the Sil River and there appeared before us a sign with a very lengthy name. I parked the car outside a bar where we saw several older men who possibly could have helped us. We were willing to ask the first person we encountered. It was then that the old man explained to us this reality: the war had left many men in the cemetery, but in the roadside ditches there were many more.

Some of the men outside the bar told us that they had on their property a grave containing the remains of two or three people, and a few even offered to come with a little tractor to open them for us. But we were looking for a larger grave that would have thirteen or fourteen bodies. We knew that the truck that took my grandfather had fifteen prisoners and that at least one of them had managed to escape.

We visited several clandestine cemeteries in fields and ditches until we ran into a man who remembered perfectly the 16th of October, 1936. He was then only twelve years old, and that night he had awakened to the sound of several gunshots, so he and his brother had run to his parents' bed. The man took us to the road and showed us the point of entry to the next town, Priaranza del Bierzo, which was just 300 meters from there. "Just before you get to the first house, you will see a turnoff to the right. They shot them right on the farm that is between the two roads. My parents did not let me go, but a lot of the school children went with the teacher to see how they buried them." Another resident of the town was accompanying us, and while he was telling Arsenio stories that he knew about other executions, I walked ahead and felt a growing anxiousness at the possibility of finding my grandfather's remains. Just as we arrived at the fork in the road, I saw a man of about seventy who was taking a stroll with his hands crossed behind his back.

---

4 The name of this town translates literally as "Free Town of the Jurisdiction."

"You must help me," I said to him. He responded calmly: "To do what?" "I am looking for a mass grave from the Civil War which contains the remains of my grandfather, along with those of a dozen other men." Then the man uncrossed his arms and pointed to a ditch at the fork and said, "They are there, under that overgrown walnut tree."

I sensed an intense emotion. I approached the tree, put my hands on the trunk and leaned into it, as if that way I could communicate with those men who had died murdered during a terrifying night so many years ago. I tried to imagine what was under that tree. Arsenio's reaction was much angrier than mine, and he cursed the assassins who had left those poor men "discarded like that, as if they were dogs." We asked the man who was helping us the name of the owner of the farm. He said that the owner had died and that from the day they buried the victims, he had never again cultivated that land, out of respect for the dead. I supposed that in an area so close to Galicia, superstition was an important factor in the relationship of the locals to the unmarked graves.[5] Afterwards, I made a note of the full name of the heir to the land, and after waiting a few minutes in silence, we left.

At that moment I had a sense of anguish, provoked by the memory of how tragic and difficult the life of my family had been since that horrible incident: the image of my grandmother who after being widowed had terrible nervous breakdowns which paralyzed her physically, surrounded by her six children who could not alert anyone at night because of the curfew. I sensed the traumatic childhood of my father, who went from being a happy child in school at ten years old to the head of the family, assuming the hardest jobs to help his siblings survive, and even thrive.

We returned to Ponferrada in the middle of the afternoon, as I had to get back to Madrid. Saying goodbye to Arsenio and thanking him for everything, I told him I would not delay in returning to interview those men and I would bring along some documentation. I could not get out of my head the image of the ditch where they had buried my grandfather. The place where he had been assassinated had just materialized along the roadside and under an outsized walnut tree. I remem-

---

5 Galicia, the northwesternmost region of Spain, is known for its culture of superstition.

bered then my grandmother who had died two years earlier—mute, silenced by a fear that had never left her since the night in which her husband handed his ring and his watch to one of his six children when he went to visit him in the prison of Villafranca del Bierzo.

2
That *Republicano* Grandfather of Mine

MY GRANDFATHER'S NAME WAS Emilio Silva Faba, and he was born in Pereje, a town in the province of Leon, in 1894. His parents' names were Rosa and Ramón. My great-grandmother was known as a very wise woman, with a very special insight. The members of my grandfather's family were farmers, and some of them emigrated to Argentina at the turn of the 20th century. Around 1915 my grandfather followed them there, and he lived for several years in Espeleta, a town close to Buenos Aires, where he worked with a cousin in a soda factory. A few years later, deciding to try his luck in the United States, he moved to New York City. He was a self-taught man, rather enlightened, who had dabbled in journalism with the publication of a few articles in newspapers such as *El Sol*[6] and other periodicals.

On June 20, 1925, my grandfather went to the immigration office of the US Department of Labor. He wanted to secure permission to be able to return to the US after visiting his hometown in Spain. His idea was to sell some property that he had inherited from his parents to have a little cash to invest in a business. In a letter that ended up with a relative living in Cuba, just prior to his trip to Spain, he wrote about opening a store in which he would sell products from Spain to the Spanish immigrants who, like he, had arrived in the city of skyscrapers. The document that was prepared for him by the US office to allow him to return contained an abundance of details to prevent anyone else from using it to enter the US. He was described as a robust man,

---

6 *El Sol* was a liberal newspaper published in Spain from 1917-1939.

dark-haired, brown eyes, 5'6 ½ and 154 lbs." In addition, the document indicated that he had a scar on his right hand, caused probably by a work injury.

Arriving from New York City to his little town in El Bierzo in the 1920's must have been quite a shock. He brought with him some material considered high tech for the times: a Kodak camera from 1914 and the first typewriter the town had ever seen. This was a model that had only one dial on a plate containing all the letters and some punctuation marks. To write on it, one had to place the iron cursor on the letter and press. It was complicated but advanced. More than once I heard my father talk about that artifact and lament that it had been lost at some point in time.

Even though the visit to Pereje had been well-organized and he had arranged his return to New York by boat from the port city of Vigo, something unexpected arose and happily changed his course: my grandmother Modesta. I do not know exactly how they met, but their first meeting must have been a beautiful spark, because my grandfather arrived in his town in July of 1925 and on the eighteenth of January of the following year, he married my grandmother when she was twenty-two years old and he ten years older. Then he made the decision to abandon his plans to return to the capital of the world; he sacrificed his American dream to live in his native land and to start anew. With the money he had saved during his years away, he rented a house and a warehouse in Villafranca del Bierzo and opened a grocery store where he sold everything from lottery tickets to utensils. The name he gave the store seemed to be the result of an advertising strategy: "La Preferida" (The Preferred Store). On a bill he sent to one of his suppliers, it said: "Food, Goods, Hardware, Coarse and Fine Salt, Chocolate and Coffee Specialties, Shoes, Slippers, Clogs, Best Pepper for Sausages, Calle del Viaducto núm. 1 (1 Viaduct Street)."

My grandparents did not have to wait long before their children were born, the first being my father, Emilio, who was born just nine months after the wedding, October 18, 1926. Ramón, Manolo, Rosario, Antonio and Carmela would follow, Carmela just three months before her father's murder.

My grandfather's business was immediately successful. They say that he was a good businessman, very kind to all, and that he had a variety of contacts who made it so that he could import certain items that his competitors could not offer. He was also a generous man who canceled the debt owed him by many families.

The proclamation of the Second Republic caused him to ally himself with the *Republicano* left, Manuel Azaña's party. His main political concern was education. In Villafranca del Bierzo, there were only religious schools, and he was determined to get a non-religious school in town and to dignify the work of the teachers who at that time were horribly paid and had very little social status in a Spain where they were in dire need. My father had a wonderful photo of those years: on the bridge of Villafranca one can see a great protest, and my father at 8 or 9 years old is holding a placard on which can be read: "We want a new school. !Viva Azaña!"

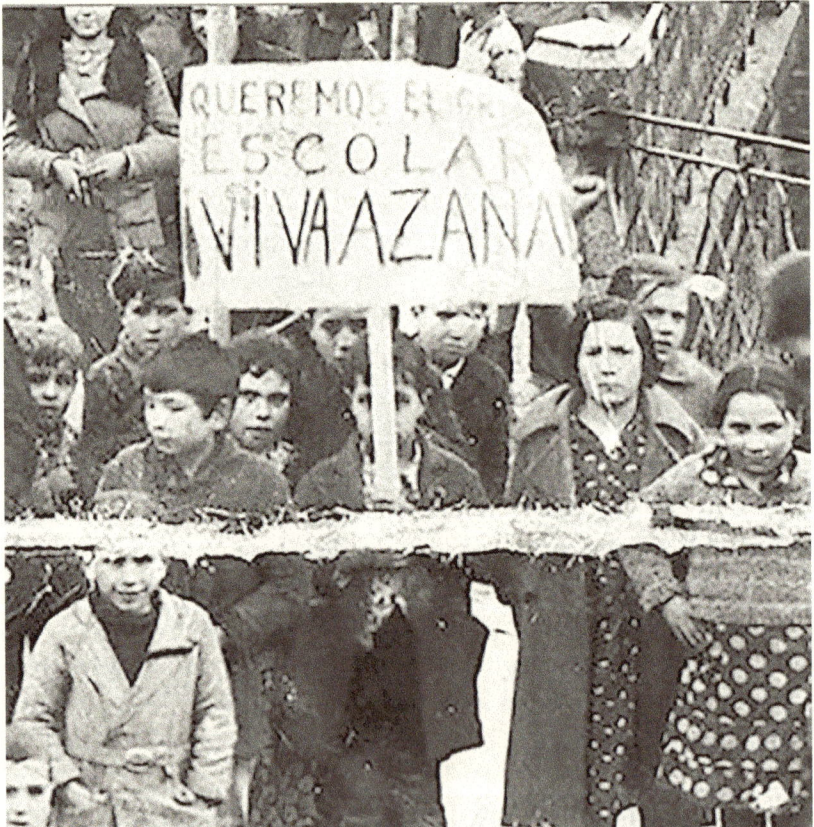

In spite of not being a candidate, my grandfather was a delegate of the party, and he became actively political. He was a moderate leftist. In 1932, a year and a half after the Second Republic was proclaimed, something happened that according to some residents of Villafranca was key to my grandfather's tragic end, although in some way his murder was unavoidable in the repressive dynamic of the right-wing insurrection.

In August of 1932, in the *Parroquial Berciana* (newspaper in El Bierzo), Antonio Carvajal y Álvarez de Toledo, one of the most powerful men in Villafranca and one with the most titles of nobility, published an article entitled, "Where Is Equality?" A few months later, my grandfather dared to publish a letter in response that ruffled some feathers in the area. After finding my grandfather's grave, I tried to locate people who had lived during the Republic, who were old enough to remember him and tell me anything they could about him. One of the people with whom I spoke was the writer Ramón Carnicer, who had two memories related to my grandfather: some very large olives that he sold in his store and the polemic of the *Parroquial Berciana*. It dealt with a dialectic contest between David and Goliath, two political visions of Spain, two models of society that not four years later awakened the anger of the giant to the point that it would impose its will by means of a war.

Parroquial Berciana, no. 983, 24 July 1932
Where Is Equality?

Equality! I hear the cry
from the hunchback Torroba,[7]
and I have to wonder,
does he want to lose the hunchback
or does he want us all to have one?"
(Manuel del Palacio)

---

7 Torroba, a common last name, rhymes with *joroba*, which means "hunchback."

Often in our times we hear the word equality, and those who tend to use this word do not understand its true meaning. All men are born equal. "Equality is one of the most precious achievements of progress," we often hear proclaimed emphatically and masterfully. Many of those who boast about their progressive ideas do not bother to analyze the word *equality* or realize that the origin of the word is none other than the excellent doctrine taught by Jesus Christ.

Sublime teaching is within reach of everyone and through which we learn that we are all brothers and sisters. In this evangelical maxim shines infinite wisdom and with this teaching—at once sublime and simple—Jesus Christ leaves the holy fire of charity lit and establishes the true and only equality that men have perverted and adulterated, giving it an additional meaning that it does not have, and with sectarian objectives trying to establish an equality that does not exist, nor ever will exist, no matter how much the modern socialist party tries to demonstrate this.

Aside from this equality that Jesus Christ preached, and which established the Christian fraternity—the foundation of all legitimate equalities—everything is inequality, and from this emanates all universal harmony and the balance of human society. With regard to the moral, the physical and the intellectual, all men are different. In all of them there are more or less notable differences.

In the material world, no two things are equal. Two drops of water, two grains of sand or two coffee grounds, seen with the aid of a microscope, even if they seem the same, have tiny differences that distinguish them and that hide from the eyes of the observer who does not look carefully. In short, Equality does not exist either physically or morally or intellectually among men anywhere. The only true Equality exists in the Gospels.

According to a famous Spanish writer of the middle of the last century,[8] "political equality, that of capitalist fortunes and dreams—from Campanella to Luis Blanc—is an aberration of thought that meanders in the dark and loses itself in chaos for

---

8 The author of this newspaper article does not reveal the name of his source.

having lost its guiding north star." If you want the strong not to oppress the weak, the rich not succumb to greed, that there be neither exploiters nor exploited, that freedom should reign without degenerating into anarchy and without authority changing into despotism, that the laws of justice be respected and that the great and the small, the learned and the unschooled, the wretched and the powerful live in harmony, love each other for the love of God, and in the spirit of grace, both the individual and the body politic will enjoy all possible happiness in this world where, through unfathomable mystery, Providence has placed us.

Completely devoid of any political passion, which so clouds our reason, and without any more information than what my own observation and experience has taught me, I have tried to develop the present theme, seen clearly through the lens of my good judgement and with moral rectitude.

I certainly realize that my limited strengths are not at all at the level required for such an important topic. Thus my humble effort may seem overly simplistic and superficial, but it may be that it serves as a stimulus for another, more accomplished and capable in this material than I, and he or she would be able to present on this topic in a more complete and profound way that could be more useful for these times in which sectarianism and false socialist doctrines seem to want to take hold of our citizenry, despite our nature.

Signed, Antonio de Carvajal y Álvarez de Toledo.

Two weeks later, the same author published again in this same newspaper.

Very few times in my life have I picked up a pen with such enthusiasm to express publicly my sincere and profound appreciation to all those who congratulated me and enjoyed my article entitled, "Where is Equality?" published recently in these columns.

This humble piece, written hurriedly, in which I expressed, albeit superficially, the concept that I have regarding true Equality, has met with frankly unexpected success. People of all social classes (both men and women), on congratulating me for this piece, have encouraged me to keep writing in this fashion, believing that I possess a competence that I do not have and honoring me in a way that is unmerited. To all, I am happy to offer my sincere thanks. It is not vanity that moves me to express myself this way. Vanity is a juvenile passion, which in youth is forgivable, as it is the age of fantasy; it would be ridiculous in the author of these lines who is in his later years.

What compels me to write here is a more noble sentiment; it is the pure satisfaction of seeing that the wave of materialism, of demoralization and disbelief that today invades our entire world, and particularly our beloved country, has not had an effect on the deep-rooted religious sentiments of the residents of Villafranca who, great lovers of tradition, have been able to keep alive the flame of our Faith.

Antonio Carvajal y Álvarez de Toledo

Parroquial Berciana, no. 985, August 28, 1932
    Open Letter To Mr. Antonio Carvajal y Álvarez de Toledo,
                From Emilio Silva Faba

My Very Dear Sir:

The principal aim of this humble letter, a bit ill-timed due to prior commitments, is to congratulate you effusively and sincerely on the article you so honorably wrote in the *Parroquial Berciana* of this historic town, entitled "Where is Equality?" At the end of that famous article, a kindred spirit to others you have written, you were kind enough to sound the alarm, inviting other better-versed writers to weigh in with more depth on the topic you developed with indisputable and well-deserved success.

I am sad to see that there has been no response to your invitation from any learned voice on this complicated matter. In light of this, and in spite of not having had the honor of meeting you personally, I am submitting this unworthy letter, with the understanding that I lack the cultural capital to engage with the subject. Nevertheless, convinced that discussion yields clarity, and sensing that I may have a penchant for writing even without the luxury of having scientific and philosophical terminology in my vocabulary, my spirit, revived and inflamed with quixotic vigor, impelled me toward this bold and rash endeavor.

With permission of the editor of the *Parroquial Berciana*, who so appropriately directs the newspaper, and with all due respect to the advanced age of Mr. Carvajal, following is my opinion on true equality.

I must take issue with certain points in your way of thinking; in some paragraphs and passages there are many lessons to learn. Those who fear Communism, Socialism and Equality should memorize those sublime lessons to which you call our attention and which you incorporate daily in all of your deeds, and they should modify, with a pinch of humanity, their archaic spirit full of avarice and egotism. With such a simple and humane method, they would put into practice the sublime teachings of Jesus Christ. Their souls, if they even have them, would stop being harsh with their peers. With that miraculous change in their hearts, we would all consider ourselves brothers and sisters, and prejudice against different groups would disappear. In a word, peace would reign, and we would all be happier. With avarice and egotism pulled out by their roots, in all of the atrophied minds, Justice would shine lavishly. In the poorest homes, turmoil would abate. With that ideal in effect, Socialists and Communists would have no cause to demand, as they do today justly, food and education for their hungry and ragged children, nor would they worry about something like Equality.

My humble opinion is that Equality should be part and parcel of our schools and universities so that all citizens may acquire the necessary culture that, sadly, the majority of Spaniards lack. This precious jewel is the solid base of people's understanding and progress, and it is a powerful weapon against those who deal in human suffering, as well as the key to navigate smoothly the unexpected twists and turns of this cruel earthly life.

By respecting each other, and by making ourselves worthy of respect as good brothers and sisters, we would all make a living from our physical, scientific or intellectual work; in this way we would free ourselves with our own efforts and not have to live off the sweat of others, and we would thus have a more humane life and a more carefree future for our old age. This is my ideal for Equality, not that of some starry-eyed do-gooders who want to force their ideas on us.

Without examining or reconsidering their deplorable and libertine pasts—for many, the cause of their often-announced unhappiness—so many people cry out for Equality. In this case, like you, Mr. Carvajal, I ask, "Where is it?" Before giving the sweat of others to the lazy slackers, they should be asked for an accounting of their lives. Depraved, lazy, dissolute.

To conclude, and so that this humble citizen who has been called a renegade may be judged however the reader wishes, I demand with all the power in my lungs and with all my might, for all Spaniards who love order and progress: Equality in the schools! Equality in the Justice system! Compassion for the downtrodden! Contempt for those who continually foment the practice of exploitation, without following God's Ten Commandments!

Hurray for the sublime teachings of the crucified Christ! And Hurray for all the citizens who practice these teachings honestly by feeding the hungry, without exploiting those who extract from the land our very necessary daily bread! And finally, Hurray for those who work sleeplessly and contribute their best for the benefit of Humanity!

With the hope that you and the other kind readers have not found herein any unintended offense, I remain,

Yours sincerely,

Emilio Silva Faba

The discovery of this letter was ineffably special to me, and it became the experience that most closely connected me to my *republicano* grandfather.

The year 1936 arrived, and general elections were held in February. My grandfather was going to work on the campaign and serve as an inspector at the polls. On February 13 of that year, Ramiro Armesto Armesto, a candidate for representative to Congress, went to the office of the attorney Virgilio Rey Amaya in the town of Vega de Espinareda in the region of El Bierzo. There he signed an affidavit for more than 60 men whom he designated as polling inspectors with the words, "To designate as inspectors and substitutes for each one of the tables and to agree with the other candidates if it were determined that a reduction in the number of inspectors would be warranted. To represent the leader in the electoral college in the use of the right that the law provides the candidates; witness the counting; file complaints; ask for the intervention of the lead attorney and have him record the minutes of the incidents that transpire; ask the authorities and their agents for their intervention and support for the free exercise of the attorney's functions; and, in general, perform all duties associated with the candidate in his absence.

This affidavit affected sixty-two men, of whom Emilio Silva Faba, a member of the *Republicano* Left, was one. It is very probable that the list was used by the Falangists who took control during the month of July, as nearly all the men whose names appeared on it were assassinated for their political ideas.

In the electoral campaign of 1936, Manuel Azaña, on his way to Galicia, stopped in Villafranca del Bierzo, at the store La Preferida. My grandfather had a conversation with him, and the presidential candidate dedicated a photograph to him, which my grandmother burned a few days after he was murdered.

During the elections of February, 1936, there occurred another seemingly minor incident which may have been a causal factor in his murder. As an inspector, my grandfather was at a table, and a cousin of my grandmother arrived to vote. She was a cloistered nun who had not even left the convent to attend her parents' funerals, yet she left the cloister to deposit her slip of paper in these elections. She appeared in full habit, accompanied by the Church authorities of Villafranca, who were many and powerful. Seeing her next to the table, my grandfather chastised her for neglecting to care for her parents in their final days. To the confrontation he had with the aristocracy of the town was added that of the Church authorities, in a town where the Grand Inquisitor Torquemada once had a palace, on Water Street. Some of the old residents of the town call the Civil War the second Inquisition. Rightly so.

3
A Tragedy Foretold

O N JULY 18, 1936, Spain devolved into a horrific situation. Hardly three days later, troops moved east into Villafranca from Galicia under the command of Comandante (Major) Manso who subdued for Franco the whole swath of Spain from the highway of La Coruña to the mountain range just to the north of Madrid. That whole area never saw a battlefront, as there was no armed resistance against the rebels whose arrival forewarned of the next three bloody years. In front of the cathedral of Villafranca was a woman who happened to see the first truckloads of soldiers approaching. Not knowing if they were *republicanos* or Franco's troops, she took a chance and raised her fist.[9] A moment later, as he watched her from his open vehicle, Major Manso silently drew his pistol and shot her in the head. The woman fell over dead. Manso ordered his driver to stop so he could ascertain his aim. Where that bloodthirsty officer stepped onto the soil of Villafranca there still stands, shamefully, a monument "To *Comandante* Manso, Liberator of This Town." The soldiers who accompanied him that day stopped several residents, which raises the suspicion that someone had been awaiting the arrival of the troops at the entrance to the town to tell them where they would find the people who should be arrested. One of the first to be detained was my grandfather, who was in his store when they entered and was quickly put in one of their trucks. That day he was lucky, because several neighborhood women from other stores, one of whom was influential in local right-wing politics,

---

9   The raised fist indicated allegiance to the political Left.

interceded for him and managed to get him released from custody. However, that convoy of prisoners went off to the hospital of San Marcos de León--one of the most notorious wartime detention and execution centers. There, soldiers would call out the names of those who were to be executed, but they would do so by calling out the most common first or last names, e.g., José or García, of which there were many, and then after an agonizing pause, they would add the missing first or last names, whereby some would be taken away and many others would be left terrified for having felt so close to death.

The Falange took control of Villafranca. They set up two jails and they occupied City Hall. My grandfather knew one of the local leaders and therefore must have thought he was not in any danger after what had happened. He had family in Argentina, and some friends told him he would be wise to go there, but he thought nothing would happen to him, that the war would not last long, and that in a few weeks everything would return to normal.

The pressure started building just a few days after the uprising. From time to time the Falange would visit La Preferida to requisition merchandise. They would take whatever they wanted and leave an IOU on the counter with a list of what they had confiscated, assuring my grandfather that the money would be paid when peace was established. Periodically they would charge him a kind of "tax." I have saved one of those documents which reads as follows:

The commission constituted to gather funds for the maintenance of the Falange militias, which are of utmost importance for the service they render protecting this town, especially at night, and to invest in the triumph of the army which represents the salvation of Spain from the hands of Russian communism, has determined that your contribution is 75 (seventy-five) pesetas, which must be remitted within three days, and for whose payment we will be very grateful.

Villafranca, August 28, 1936
Enrique Gómez, Mayor
Signing for the Commission

The "we will be very grateful" was in lieu of saying, "you won't be in the next truck headed to your grave." No one knows how many of these slips of paper were needed to safeguard his life, but what is certain is that the family money was disappearing quickly, putting my grandfather in danger.

In the months of August, September and October, the Falangists of Villafranca were systematic in the harsh application of cleaning up the rearguard of what they called the Anti-Spain. According to official documents, 162 civilians were executed. The strategy may have been to assassinate first those with few resources, leaving alive the leftists who could more easily finance the campaign to exterminate Russian communism.

On October 16, 1936, Emilio Silva Faba was called to City Hall, apparently to sign another promissory note or make another actual payment. His son Ramón walked with him as far as the door to the building. Before entering, the *republicano* businessman said goodbye to him and told him to return home. Neither of the two knew they would never see each other again, in spite of the fact that clearly something was awry; that night he was detained in the place that the locals called "the jail of the accused."

At nightfall, his wife Modesta appeared at the front door of City Hall, accompanied by her son Manuel. They were bringing Emilio a change of clothes and some dinner. The guard only allowed Manuel to enter, while she remained outside in agony over the fate of her husband. At that moment, Emilio must have known what awaited him, because he handed this third son of his a watch on a chain and his wedding ring inscribed with his initials.

The young Manuel said goodbye to his father, left the building, and showed his mother what he had been given. On seeing the watch and the ring, Modesta was overcome by a sense of doom. She asked herself to whom she could turn to save her husband, and she knew that she had to move swiftly, as she was aware of detainees being taken away and executed without warning along the local roads. She took her son home and went to visit one of the men who had the kind of influence that could save lives. He was a local businessman and, currently, mayor of the town of Villafranca. Modesta Santín, kneeling next to the counter of his store, her eyes bathed in tears out of fear and desperation, begged him to save her husband, a good man who had never hurt anyone. While my grandmother beseeched him for help, the mayor, unmoved, never stopped placing small objects on a shelf, without deigning to look at her. Modesta left there, convinced that only a miracle could prevent the impending tragedy.

The next morning, the family's oldest son (also named Emilio and who happens to be my father), went over to the City Hall with another change of clothes and some breakfast for his father. On arriving at the door, he told one of the guards that he wanted to give a few things to his father. With a sinister smile, the armed man who was guarding the entrance responded that his father was no longer there, that perhaps he had jumped out a window and escaped. Often have I thought of the coldness of that man. What enjoyment could he have found in making fun of a child who, without knowing it, had just lost his father, and who would soon go from being a happy ten-year old student to a low-level road worker or a shepherd on a lonely hillside?

When that child returned home with that terrible piece of news, my grandmother went into hysterics and the family began to mobilize to try to recover the body. One of the first people that the family visited was the local priest. My grandmother begged him to intercede for her to discover where her husband's body was located, but the priest simply told her that he was where he deserved to be.

Two of Modesta's brothers, Marcelino and Saturio, rented a car and went from town to town in the region in search of any clue that could point them to the site of the execution. They drove many miles and came across several bodies, the result of other executions that had taken place the previous night. Returning from their first long day of searching, they spoke of the murder of a woman and her baby boy whose testicles they had cut off and shoved into his mouth. Many years later, I heard the same story in Priaranza del Bierzo from a resident who told me how a superior officer had learned of that atrocity, discovered the Falangist who had committed it, and ordered him to cease the killings. That may have saved the lives of some people who were on the "hit" list.

The following morning, they resumed their search and passed through Priaranza del Bierzo. The day before, fourteen men had been buried in a common grave, one of whom fit the description of Emilio Silva Faba. Modesta's brothers spoke with one of the young people who, for having been a member of the Socialist Youth, was forced to bury the bodies.

The events that culminated with the death of Emilio Silva Faba and thirteen other men in a ditch at the entrance to Priaranza del Bierzo have been reconstructed with the help of different testimonials in a type of horrific *Alexandria Quartet*. The jail cell in the Villafranca City Hall on that 16th day of October, 1936 was filled to capacity. At night, an Olarte gaseosa[10] truck and a car with four gunmen stopped in front of the mayor's office. Several prisoners were loaded into the truck which immediately headed east toward Ponferrada, followed by the vehicle with the four armed Falangists. Along the way they stopped at least once because one of the men assassinated that night was in his underwear and it was believed that he was taken from his bed and thrown into the truck with the other prisoners.

In Ponferrada the truck picked up at least one person, Juan Francisco Falagán, the son of a Civil Guard whom the local Falangists did not want to kill to spare themselves problems, preferring to hand him over to those of Villafranca. During the excavation process, a granddaughter of Juan Francisco Falagán approached the site claiming that in it were the remains of her grandfather. At first, it seemed that since he was not from Villafranca he could not be there. However, she put me in touch with Aureliano Sánchez, a man who was riding his bike around Priaranza the night of the execution.

"I heard some shots, but I didn't know where they had come from until I rounded a bend and saw a truck and a car with the headlights on, and I hid behind a blackberry bush while they finished shooting them. I waited until the vehicles left, and when I went close to the ditch, I heard that one of them was moving. The next morning, I returned to see fourteen corpses, and suddenly a man approached riding

---

10 *Gaseosa* is a sweet, carbonated drink, usually without any additional flavor, which is sometimes added to wine in the summer.

a bicycle and turned the bodies over so that he could see the faces until he found one he identified as the son of Falagán, the Civil Guard."

This testimony helped explain why they would have taken the prisoners 30 kilometers outside of Villafranca, at night, and along a road in terrible condition.

The convoy of death then proceeded toward Priaranza del Bierzo along the Orense highway. My grandfather was seated near the door and facing Leopoldo Moreira, a neighbor from Trabadelo, who proposed to him that they try to escape as soon as the Falangists started to remove the heavy canvas cover of the truck. My grandfather was forty-two years old, not very physically fit, and not confident that he could flee successfully, which is why he rejected the offer. At the entrance to Priaranza, the truck and car stopped with the headlights on, and as soon as the covering of the truck was removed, two prisoners, hands tied, jumped out and ran. The gunmen did not have their weapons drawn, and it took them a few seconds to begin shooting. Those shots awakened the neighbors. Of the two fugitives, one was quickly felled by gunfire, and the other managed to disappear into the darkness. Leopoldo Moreira ran without stopping, unable to see anything but knowing that behind him was looming a certain somber death. He spent the night running but still heard how his companions each received two bullets to the head. His frenzied steps took him to the edge of a river, which he crossed blindly, and when he reached the other shore, he kept running. In the middle of the night, he had to cross another river, and by dawn he saw that his bad fortune had brought him back to the place from which he had escaped. He had crossed the Sil River twice and had awakened at the site of the execution.

In the daylight he was able to find his way to his hometown of Pereje, my grandparents' village, with his clothes in shreds and his body covered with bruises. A brother of Arsenio, the man who had accompanied me to search for the unmarked grave, was the first person to see him. He hid him in a hayloft and gave him some food and clean clothes.

Leopoldo survived in the mountains near his town until August 16, 1937, when he was arrested by the Falange and summarily executed by being shot so many times in the face that he was unrecognizable to the people who were asked to identify the body. By chance, before his capture, he was able to tell several people about what happened the night his fellow prisoners were killed. One of those was my grandmother who met with him when Leopoldo's mother invited her to her home after running into her at a local fair. Modesta Santín kept secret and in the deepest part of her heart every word that she heard at that clandestine meeting.

Emilio Silva Faba had died with thirteen other men. During the ride in the truck, he had asked to be the first one killed because he did not want the last things seen by his eyes to be the executions of his comrades. Seconds before his death, he asked one of the gunmen, whom he knew, to please not kill him because he would be leaving behind his wife with six children to raise alone. The gunman responded that they would all be fine, and he pulled the trigger of the handgun twice, shattering his skull at close range.

Often over the years I have thought of the fear my grandfather must have felt in those hours, the fear that the other men, too, must have felt on being herded toward the slaughterhouse. Fear for their own lives, fear for those they would leave helpless, the uncertainty of not knowing if that punishment that was being meted out to them would also be directed at other members of their families. More than once have I closed my eyes and tried to put myself in their place, to sense the same anguish, the same helplessness, the same panic.

The reconstruction of those events came from several sources in addition to the mother of the escapee Leopoldo Moreira. Several years after the crime, one of my uncles, Ramón, began working as an apprentice in a mechanic shop in Villafranca. For him, it was a good opportunity to be able to learn a trade and be able to contribute to his household. One day, a friend of the owner told Ramón that he wanted to speak to him in private. They decided to meet one afternoon, during which the friend told my uncle that the owner of the shop was the man who was driving the truck the night his father and the other men were killed. He added that the owner had been threatened into doing this. The friend then told Ramón that the owner had told him approximately where it had happened. Ramón had accompanied my grandfather to the City Hall the evening he was arrested.

Several months later he had to repair the car of Antonio de Carvajal y Álvarez de Toledo, the man whom my grandfather had debated in the *Parroquial Berciana*, and he told Ramón that he had had nothing to do with his father's death.

As the years passed, Ramón and his siblings gathered fragments of the event—phrases that were overheard, insinuations by people who may have known something—and they started solving part of the puzzle. A part of this story is probably skewed due to fear, desire, and the need to get answers.

I returned home after locating the unmarked grave of my grandfather. What could I do? I had heard my father mention his mother's wish to be buried next to her husband, but how could those bones be recovered?

As soon as I arrived home, I called my father to tell him that I had been with Arsenio and that together we had found the grave, as if I had discovered that place, as if I had been the first descendant to step next to that overgrown walnut tree. But this story is riddled with fears and silences, and the news I thought I had was not even close to a revelation. That place already had been visited by a number of family members without my ever knowing it.

The first to visit that site was my father, in the 1950's. One day, while working in the power plant in Ponferrada, he rented a bicycle and rode around the area where his father was said to have been killed. In those days, one could not appear in a town and begin asking questions without raising uncomfortable suspicion, so my father looked carefully in the ditches for some indication that he had found the spot. He remembered having sat down at the entrance to Priaranza when two civil guards came along and asked him what business he had there. My father assumed that he had been labeled a "son of a *rojo* ("red," or leftist, sometimes considered communist)," so, to avoid problems, he got back on the bike and rode away without saying a word.

The second member of the family to visit the site was Manolo, a few months after the death of Franco. The son who was the last person to see Emilio Silva Faba alive went to Priaranza del Bierzo to ask about the grave. The man who had owned the farm in 1936 was still alive, and with his help my uncle drew a map with details of the roads and trees from that year, and he was able to pinpoint the location of the grave. On the third day, digging with an excavator, when we encountered the first of the remains, Manolo took out of his pocket the hand-drawn map and saw that it was, in fact, correct.

The third was my uncle Ramón, who, when I found the grave, had been pondering who the other men in the grave could have been, and he was visiting local archives in search of the list so that he could make contact with their families.

The journey had begun. The desire to recover those remains and give them a dignified burial next to the tomb of my grandmother was the journey I was to take. At times I have the feeling that everything was already prepared for me. The way in which events unfolded from that moment on, and the individuals who became involved in the work, seemed to have been waiting for a spark to set in motion the process of restoring the dignity and memory of those who had constructed our first democracy.

4
A Hole in the Silence

ON SUNDAY, OCTOBER 8, 2000, a two-page article was published in the newspaper *La Crónica de León*, in the section on "El Bierzo," entitled, "My Grandfather Was Also One of the Disappeared." I had written it a few days earlier, thinking that it could be of some use to the family members of the other victims in the Priaranza grave who might want to contact me. I made a conscious effort to associate our Civil War victims to the "disappeared" of Argentina and Chile. I began this way: "I am the grandson of a *desaparecido*. My grandfather's name was Emilio Silva Faba. They shot him to death next to thirteen other people and they left him in a roadside ditch at the entrance to Priaranza del Bierzo. His funeral services consisted of a hole in the ground and a few spadefuls of dirt under which his body remains today." And it ended as follows: "His remains can rest in the place his family chooses. I knew that there was a story to tell, and that is what I have done. But my story is a tiny piece of a greater story. There are many unmarked mass graves full of unidentified men."

One detail at the end of the text turned out to be fundamental. Underneath the final line was my phone number, in case a family member of an unidentified victim wanted to call.

The following day, around 4:00 in the afternoon, the telephone rang, a call that was going to alter the direction of my life. It was from Julio Vidal, an archaeologist from León, who knew from childhood the existence of the grave. His mother was from Priaranza, and from the time he was a little boy playing outside with his friends, whenever they came close to what they called the "haunted spot," they would run away quickly, as they would from any other place that gave them reason to be afraid. Julio explained to me that when he became an archaeologist, more than once he thought about the possibility of excavating that site to try to find out about the men who were buried there. More than once he mentioned this possibility to his wife, María Encina, a forensic anthropologist. Thus, when they read the article in the newspaper, they decided to call me.

Until that day, I had the idea of doing the excavation with my uncle Ramón, trying not to break the bones and lifting the bodies out one by one. I had no clear idea of what I was saying when I thought of that. Everything changed when Julio Vidal offered to carry out the exhumation of the remains with the help of other archaeologists.

On October 21, 2000, around 5:30 p.m., the bucket of a backhoe opened up the earth at the burial site of those who later would be known as the Priaranza Thirteen. It was a rainy day, cold and unpleasant. Julio Vidal was directing the work of the digger operator. Several residents of the town were watching expectantly from the sidewalk in front. From time to time, one of them would approach to give his or her opinion on where they thought the remains would be found.

The evening closed without any sign of the bodies. The following morning, very early, the work resumed. A number of people had arrived to help with the exhumation, some of whom related stories from their parents or grandparents. Among those who came was Isabel González Losada, an eighty-three-year-old woman from the town of Palacios del Sil, whose brother Eduardo was buried in an unmarked grave at the entrance to Piedrafita de Babia. Another person was Aníbal, a man in his forties who had watched the excavation for the first two days without a word.

Again, the next day there were no remains visible. We started to deal with the possibility that they could have been under the asphalt of the road that had been widened by more than a meter on each side since the year of the execution. That day, we had a special visitor— Francisco Cubero, an eighty-five-year-old man whom the Falangists had forced, along with two other boys from Villalibre, to bury the bodies due to their participation in the Socialist Youth. This was to be a "teaching moment" in that the boys could see what was in store for them if they continued their political involvement.

Francisco's arrival at the excavation site was impactful. A few days before, I had visited him at his house, and he had told me his story. It happened that the morning after the execution in 1936, the falangists went to look for Francisco. They told him to follow them with a pick and shovel, and they took him to the place selected for the burial where they told him and the two other youths to start digging. People were gathering around the scene, including school children, neighbors and others who were walking by or on bikes.

They dug a grave that was twenty-six feet long, five feet wide, and two and one-half feet deep. They deposited the fourteen bodies in the grave and returned to their homes. Two days later, the family of one of the murdered men (whose identity I never learned) arrrived in town and paid one of Cubero's companions ten *duros* (a handsome sum for the times) to dig up their relative. The boys remembered him easily, as he was the one who was arrested and shot in his underwear.

Cubero arrived at the excavation site and the backhoe was stopped. Many years had passed since he had buried the bodies and the geography in his mind was confused. He identified the burial site as a place on the farm that had already been excavated, and people were becoming disheartened. The following morning the work resumed, and at about 11:00 a.m., the backhoe operator announced that he had just noticed a change in the density of the earth when he drove the bucket into it. When he raised it back up, there was a boot on the ground. Immediately the archaeologist began sifting through the dirt, and next to the boot were the bones of a foot. The grave was less than 8 inches from the first trench that had been dug, and we had the good fortune of finding the first human foot of the line of bodies without damaging any of them.

That was a very emotional moment and difficult to put into words. I had tried on several occasions to imagine what I would feel when the bodies were unearthed. I had tried to rationalize it, but when that boot appeared, that object that signaled the discovery of human remains, emotion trumped reason. At once I remembered the inscription that my grandmother had ordered for a family vault which she had bought only a few years earlier and on which my grandfather's last names appeared; this was her way of holding onto the hope that one day their remains would rest together.

Among so many other feelings, I sensed a kind of sad satisfaction, compensating for the tension of the two previous days. We were beginning to put things in order, to obtain a little island of historic justice in the middle of an ocean of oblivion for those men who, with their political ideas and hard work, had built the first democratic society to have existed in Spain.

Since it was Sunday, the disinterment was suspended until the following weekend. A group of archaeologists and medical examiners willing to volunteer on this project were awaiting a phone call from Julio Vidal so they could begin to help.

Returning to Madrid, I called the Subdelegation of the Government of León to request police protection for the night the grave would remain open with the remains visible, so that no harm would come to them. Daniel Fernández, the mayor of Priaranza, sent a fax from city hall to convert the request into an official demand. The protection was granted, to the surprise of many who found it ironic to see the Civil Guard caring for the remains of a group of "rojos" (leftists).

On Friday, October 27, Julio Vidal supervised the work at the grave site, specifically, the grading of the ground to prepare it for the next day's excavation. On Saturday, the excavation began with the help of a group of experts, including three archaeologists (Vidal himself, Mari Luz González and Venancio Carlón); a forensic anthropologist (María Encina Prada); a leading medical examiner (Francisco Etxebarría), and several assistants.

That same day, in the pages of the newspaper *Diario de León*, in the edition dealing with El Bierzo, there appeared an article written by Julio Vidal and María Encina Prada explaining the reasons for their commitment to the opening of the grave in Priaranza.

"Archaeology of Reconciliation"
Contemporary Archaeology, or Archaeology of the recent past, has become in recent years a principal topic of current affairs and controversy in neighboring countries. For example, in France in

1991, the archaeological excavation of the World War I mass grave of Saint Rémy-la-Calonne, to recover the body of Alain Fournier (a gifted French author who was executed along with twenty other soldiers by German troops on the battlefront of Meuse in the summer of 1914) was not without heated debate between archaeologists and anthropologists; the archaeologists were distrusting of the characterization of the work as an "archaeological intervention." This is easily understood, given that archaeologists generally can be impartial to their findings since they are so far removed in time and therefore anonymous. Not in this case, when we have at hand such a fresh memory. Furthermore, political authorities invariably try to cash in on these matters. The then Minister of Culture, Jack Lang, as well as mayor of Blois, a nearby town, rushed to offer political support for the excavation of the grave, hoping to gain points (votes) in the court of public opinion. Something similar, without the distances, especially chronological, has occurred recently in Spain with a surprising solitary archaeological excavation in Madrid, in the Plaza de Ramales, intended to discover the body of the painter Velázquez. The Community of Madrid has spent millions on what is really a show of political power.

"Archaeology of the Recent Past" provokes—why not say it?— unease, in addition to deep emotions unavoidably tied to the proximity of events with which it deals. This fact has been heralded by the work of the Argentine forensic team which specialized in the study of common and individual unmarked graves resulting from the violations of human rights committed in Argentina during its last military dictatorship (1976-1983). Add to this the study of many others—in El Salvador, Perú, Chile, Rwanda, Croatia, Bosnia, etc., so many places—by anthropologists, medical examiners and archaeologists, with the aim of helping judges and tribunals to exhume the buried bodies of victims, indelible and dramatic witnesses to the unending human capacity for brutality.

Sixty-four years ago, in the middle of the night on October 16, 1936, fourteen men were assassinated in the outskirts of Priaranza del Bierzo and buried in a common grave at the edge of a road. Without any doubt, they all died simply for defending ideas that only a few months earlier were completely in line with the reigning constitutional and democratic framework of their society. It seems that almost all of them were taken from the municipal jail cell in Villafranca, where they were held due to the repression that followed the Francoist military uprising three months earlier. These "disappeared" men, after a genuine, prolonged and crushing military coup, constituted the first line of one of the most sordid and terrible pages in the history of Spain. For three years, hundreds of thousands of Spaniards, from both sides of the conflict, would lose their lives or suffer imprisonment and other hardships. Many of those on the losing side had no choice but to emigrate. These events led to a sinister dictatorship, a form of government which goes hand in hand with Totalitarian regimes—Nazism and Fascism—which have led the world to the worst confrontations it has seen. This dictatorship would last forty years, leaving our nation literally outside of the western world.

Everyone in Priaranza knows of the existence of this mass grave. Even the mayor of the town at the time, Blas López, was murdered in similar circumstances. This happened in other towns of the Bierzo, as well. They are all a well-known secret, subject always to a pervasive and terrified silence. These mass graves should no longer represent the shameful conscience of a transition to democracy. As long as they continue to be covered up, that frightful page of our history will not have ended. They must be catalogued and protected, and even made into commemorative monuments against intolerance and brutality. And our Public Administration, instead of looking the other way, should help both financially and technologically. For the descendants who want to properly inter their relatives who are buried there, rather than a source of confrontation, this could be a symbol of reconciliation among Spaniards.

As archaeologists and anthropologists, we know that the matter at hand is not exactly "archaeological" because the graves do not constitute in the strictest sense, pure research; what they could contribute to the improvement of the historical knowledge of those events would place it in the realm of the insignificant, since it deals with well-known facts. However, Archaeology can help, with its techniques, to fulfill the long-held desires of those who yearn to recover their relatives. In fact, the careful exhumation of the bones—if they are naturally preserved—will pave the way to facilitate their anthropological study. The collaboration of both disciplines—Archaeology and Anthropology—will allow for the recovery, in the best possible condition, of the bodies and the sundries associated with them, providing a first individual assessment and then later, in the laboratory, attempting a more exact identification, including the name, thanks to the information that the relatives may provide: age, physical characteristics, illnesses they may have suffered, etc., all according to a rigorously followed protocol. Finally, if these standard methods of identification fail, we may resort to DNA testing.

What has encouraged us to help the efforts of Emilio Silva Faba's family to recover his body and those of his fellow prisoners from the mass grave in Priaranza has been an almost professional motivation, in particular, to avoid mistakes in the excavation, for example the one made recently in Arganza in which an excavating machine was used. We are only going to use that kind of machine to remove the surface dirt that covers an unmarked grave.

But we have also been encouraged by a firm will to recognize and remember the executed, victims of horrific events which, for that reason alone, we must never forget.

The man who had come to observe the scene at the gravesite the week earlier and remained silent throughout, Aníbal, once again came to the excavation. I greeted him, thinking that perhaps he was a relative of one of the victims. Until then we had only been able to identify four of the men, and only with the help of my uncle Ramón who had gone almost door to door in the nearby towns to get information. But Aníbal had no relative, at least not in that grave. His grandfather, Aníbal Arroyo Buitrón, was from Toreno, another town in the area, and he had been executed. However, the fear-inspired silence imposed on that family turned the tragedy into a taboo which, until now, no one had dared break.

Something very powerful happened next to the grave. The thread of memory began to weave together stories and people who from that point on became vital to the process, dedicating their time, their efforts and their talents to drill through the fear and the silence. And so, through those holes in the ground, so many men and women who died unjustly will return from oblivion.

The process of exhumation showed me the importance of the use of archaeological methods in opening the graves. While the archaeologists were carrying out their tasks, the assistants were sifting through the dirt to find any little detail: human remains, buttons from clothing, or bullets from 9 mm handguns that were used in the killings.

By late afternoon on Sunday, twelve bodies had been unearthed. Around the grave we debated about the thirteenth; perhaps it had been removed by relatives without anyone knowing. When the archaeologists lifted the remains of the twelfth body, a hand of the thirteenth appeared, and the remains of this victim were exhumed the following week.

All the remains were placed in a multi-use building belonging to the government of Priaranza. The next week, the anthropologist and the medical examiner studied them to try to find clues that would help identify them. We had mentioned the possible use of DNA testing, but first the forensic report had to be written to try to match the information brought by the few family members whom we knew.

5
Thousands of Nameless Men

MY UNCLE RAMÓN VISITED several historical archives to locate a list of the names of the thirteen men we disinterred and to contact the families of those victims. He went to Ponferrada, León, Salamanca and Oviedo. They would send him from one place to the next without giving him any hope of finding the information he needed in any official center. Finally, they sent him to the Military Archives in El Ferrol, under the auspices of the Military Tribunal Number 4 of A Coruña.

They had told my uncle by phone that finding the information he was seeking would be complicated. The archive was full of files, but not in good order. When I called the same office, the person who spoke with me told me that there were nearly 12,000 cases, individual and collective, just from the province of León. That meant that the file in which the list of the Priaranza Thirteen might be found would be a single file. Additionally, the multiple-person cases were labeled with only one name, as well as the total number of people who were part of that same case. It was entirely possible that none of the six names that we had so far was on the cover of the file. Furthermore, they still had not made a list of all the names included in each file, including those that were not on the covers of the files.

They explained to us that they had started the work of listing all the names in all the files, and that they would finish the work in six or seven years—enough time for the generation that lived the Civil War to be erased. We then suggested the possibility of going there to do the research ourselves; they said that this was impossible, that it was a restricted archive, and that what we needed to do was give the names of the victims we had identified to the department known as "Amnesties."

The way things work in the military archives in Spain is one of the great indicators of the presence of surrealism in recent history. More than sixty years after the end of the war, there are still tens of thousands of documents that, because they fall under military jurisdiction, cannot be consulted by family members or researchers. In the United States, compromising information is often declassified after twenty-five years. Here in Spain, there seemed to exist a strategy to delay the availability of that type of information and keep it out of the hands of our society.

Nevertheless, we handed in a list of names and a few months later received the file of a certain Juan Uría, the namesake of one of those who may have been among the Priaranza Thirteen and who, though he personally had no connection to the unmarked grave, was in fact connected to that history. Juan Uría had been imprisoned. He was doing his required military service when the war broke out, but his ideas did not align with those of the Francoist side. During a military Mass, Uría leaned on the bars of his cell and began singing the communist anthem, the "Internationale." He was court-martialed. Included in the file were the accusation and the defense. He claimed he thought the song was a military march, and that it should not have been made into such a big deal because he only sang a few of the stanzas. He was sentenced to death and was executed a few days later. At the end of the file was a statement from a neighbor of his who described who Juan Uría was, his political views, his associates, his relatives, and other information.

Imagining those thousands of personal stories in the hands of historians was something that was going to evolve into a cause. Later we learned that some of those files contained personal effects: letters that prisoners had written to their families, photographs of their wives and/or children, etc. These were things that held emotional value, things that families never had a chance to recover.

It must be noted that in the twenty-five years since the end of the dictatorship and the beginning of democracy, the families have never been contacted to offer them any information. There has never been an accounting of the dead or "disappeared" whereby people in small towns without financial means or social contacts could get information from their local governments. I still recall how in the National Newspaper Archives, the newspapers during and after the war were frayed and almost illegible due to the hundreds of hands that had used them to search among the names of those arrested or wounded to be able to secure the pensions given to *republicano* soldiers or their widows during the war.

The week after the exhumation of the twelve bodies—the thirteenth had not yet been recovered—the forensic studies began. María Encina Prada and Francisco Extebarría prepared a report on each one of them for the purpose of being able to identify them. Although November 20, 2000, was the twenty-fifth anniversary of the death of Franco, our attention was on working against the injustices that were committed during the transition to democracy. That day the magazine *Interviu* published a report entitled "The Priaranza Thirteen," a detailed article on the excavation and search for our relatives. A telephone number was included in the article. We began receiving calls from different parts of the nation, which highlighted the true scope of the problem. In October, the same magazine had published a report entitled, "More Unmarked Graves than in Yugoslavia," which covered different parts of Spain: Oviedo, Mérida, Priaranza, etc.

6

Recovering Memory

SOME WEEKS AFTER THE exhumation in Priaranza del Bierzo, I met Santiago Macías. In spite of his youth, he had spent years gathering information about the Civil War, interviewing old people and restoring photographs for them with the enthusiasm of a historian, without having direct family involvement. We both were very interested in the subject, and we were willing to get deeply involved in the work. For that reason we decided to create the Association for the Recovery of Historical Memory.

We registered the association with the Ministry of the Interior, very much aware that the problem of the unmarked graves was not something that was pertinent only to the area of El Bierzo. I had done substantial reading on the victims of the Franco repression, and I knew of a number of friends who had lost their grandparents to the violence. But as we began to trace a line between the dead who were buried in cemeteries and those who were in unmarked graves, we realized that this was something that affected thousands of families.

That same December, thanks to the proposal made by Daniel Fernández, the mayor of Priaranza, the governing council of El Bierzo approved a resolution to help with the exhumation of mass graves of the Civil War. The twenty-four representatives from the Partido Socialista del Obrero Español or PSOE (Spanish Socialist Workers' Party), and the twenty-three from the Partido Popular (conservative party) voted unanimously to support this effort. The resolution provided for help with the research and with the return of recovered remains to family members. It was, for us, a very symbolic gesture, because it was the first time that political power took a stand on this issue.

Six weeks after presenting the statutes, we received confirmation from the Ministry of the Interior that they had been approved. During the first months of the year 2001, we began to compile information and design a strategy for achieving the objectives we had laid out.

The next exhumation we performed was in Fresnedo on September 8, 2001. This concerned a mass grave of three men and one woman, Isabel Picorel, the mother of Vicente Moreira, one of the so-called "children of the war."[11] The search for the remains with the excavator took more than three days until finally they were visible and exhumed by the same experts who had worked, without charging a penny, in Priaranza.

Vicente Moreira recalled the day when his mother, his two brothers and he had to flee their town after someone warned them that they were about to be arrested. They spent the night of their escape curled up in some wild shrubs on a nearby mountain. The next morning, Isabel Picorel returned to her home to get a few things and never returned. Vicente fled with one of his brothers toward Asturias where his father was being held prisoner. From there they took a boat to the Soviet Union. Vicente studied Fine Arts and returned to Spain in 1956.

A year after the death of Franco, Vicente Moreira mustered the courage to locate the exact place where his mother was killed. The owner of the farm in question did not dare approach the place he knew to be the site of the grave, but stayed just over two hundred yards back, pointing in the direction Vicente needed to walk. When he got Vicente to the right spot, on which for years he had prevented his cattle from grazing, he moved his arm excitedly.

On hearing that common graves were being opened in El Bierzo, Vicente Moreira sent a letter to the mayor of Cubillos del Sil, José Luis Ramón, asking for help in disinterring the remains of his mother. On reading the letter, the mayor, feeling particularly moved, lent his immediate support for the research of the grave and the removal of the

---

11   Children who were evacuated to other countries at the beginning of the Spanish Civil War.

bodies. In the letter, Moreira described the harsh story that led to his becoming an orphan.

Letter to the Government of Cubillos del Sil
from Vicente Moreira Picorel

During the first days of the Civil War, my father, Ramón Moreira Justel, along with several companions, mostly miners, began walking toward Asturias to defend the legitimate, elected government of the Republic. My mother, Isabel Picorel Celada, my brothers Valentín and Ramón, and I stayed at home, without a father or any financial support.

I was eleven years old, and I remember the day the Falangists arrived in Langre, where we lived. They came via the Sierra del Rozo in the second half of the month of August, 1936, firing their weapons as they approached the town. I remember running toward the mountain until nightfall, when I met up with my family. It was then that I learned that my mother's life had been threatened. For this reason, and in order not to leave her children orphaned, she had no choice but to flee. We spent the night in the house of a neighbor in Langre, Cipriano Alonso Campillo. In the wee hours of the next morning, we headed out with the idea of skirting the town to take the road toward Sorbeda, but the first rays of the sun prevented this by illuminating the whole area. Then we just took off running without any direction to get out of that hell. We spent that day walking around the mountain, and at night we slept in the heather. I remember that my mother put her arms around me and held me to keep me warm on that cold August night. The following morning, we finally made it to Sorbeda and were given shelter in the home of friends of my parents, Tomás Ruiz and his wife, Benigna.

At dusk, my mother, in spite of the threats, decided to return to Langre with my brother Valentín to pick up some things from our abandoned home—clothes and some other things we would need to be able to make the trip to Asturias, which was still under government control. But on arriving in San Miguel de Langre, they were arrested and taken to Toreno del Sil. It was the 26th of August.

The next day, Cipriano Alonso Campillo, the neighbor who had given us shelter that first night in Langre, was also arrested. The Falangists had also summoned other people, including Sergio Rodríguez Prieto and his cousin Bernardino Carro Prieto. Others who knew they were going to be summoned managed to escape, including my brother Valentín, who headed to Sorbeda to meet up with us.

In the middle of the night on August 28, a light truck left Toreno del Sil for Ponferrada. In it were Isabel Picorel Celada, my mother, forty-two years old; Cipriano Alonso Campillo, forty-four; Sergio Rodríguez Prieto, twenty-seven, from Tombrio de Arriba; and Bernardino Carro Prieto, twenty-one, from the same town.

When they reached the the town of Fresnedo, they were made to get out of the vehicle and in a meadow next to a spring at the edge of town they were killed. The next day, the father of one of the young men who was killed, on seeing that his son had not returned home, mounted a horse and rode to Toreno del Sil. Before arriving, someone he knew stopped him and told him that he had heard gunshots during the night near Fresnedo. The father went to the fateful place and beheld, shocked and dismayed, the four bodies lying in the meadow. They remained there until some of the residents of the town were forced to bury them in that very spot.

It is necessary to remember, too, the names of the assassins who terrorized and sacked the area, including the De Paz brothers: Rogelio, Manuel, Gerardo, Avelino and Andrés; Fausto Fernández, who killed 104 people; Pepe "the Maragato"[12] who was a cousin of the De Paz brothers; and Severino Castro, the son of the chief engineer Castro. Several priests who collaborated with the Falangists "by the grace of God" are also "worthy" of remembering, including Fr. Paciano and Fr. Gonzalo.

---

12 The Maragato people are a genetically isolated human group living in the area around Astorga, NW Spain.

When Asturias fell to the fascists in 1937, my father was arrested and condemned to death, but he managed to have his sentence changed to a four-year prison term. After my mother was killed, my brothers and I were sent to the USSR, returning some years later. Throughout my life, and especially in the most difficult times, I have thought about how I could recover my mother's body, to once again, in this unjust world, feel warmth in her presence, as on the night in August of 1936 when she cradled me in her arms against the cold. To do this, I plan to appeal to the Association for the Recovery of Historical Memory, whose humanitarian work deserves unconditional support.

The mayor of Cubillos del Sil contacted us and asked for our help in opening the grave in Fresnedo. His office gave us a stipend which allowed Santiago Macías to work for three months to search all the records in the Bierzo region with the aim of preparing the first census of victims of the Civil War in the region.

Until the exhumation in Fresnedo, any media that published information relating to the excavation of unmarked graves was local. On that occasion, a national newspaper, *El País*, published half a page, and three foreign correspondents came to witness the work of the archaeologists: one from German public television, ARD; one from the German left-wing newspaper *Tageszeitung*; and one from the Dutch newspaper *NRC*. For two days they patiently watched the work of the backhoe while we explained to them that the delay was a direct consequence of the fear suffered by the people during the Franco regime and that the change to democracy had not assuaged that fear, a fear that had prevented residents from indicating the exact place where they knew the four bodies were buried. The foreign correspondents also spoke with the family members and people from surrounding towns and villages, and they expressed surprise at how harsh the situation in Spain had been and how silent people were in spite of the almost twenty-six years that had passed since the dictator's death.

In the final months of the year 2000, we received some letters and quite a number of telephone calls from different parts of Spain in which many people told us about their search for a "disappeared" family member. We had a list of the common graves in El Bierzo and of people who were hoping for the opportunity to be able to recover the remains of their relatives. There was no doubt that Spain was one large mass grave.

In January of 2002 we set up a page on the Internet on a server that offered space for free, and we designed it using Pagebuilder, a simple design tool. A slow trickle of visitors to the page began to contact us via email. The exhumed remains of the Priaranza Thirteen continued to be housed in the building held by the local government in hopes that some laboratory would be able to do the DNA testing to try to identify them. In addition to restoring their identity, we wanted to create a precedent in Spain, providing a complete model of how to perform an exhumation, beginning with the work of the archaeologists, followed by that of the medical examiners and ending, if necessary, with more advanced methods in the techniques of identification.

At the same time, we made contact with José Antonio Lorente, Professor of Legal Medicine at the University of Granada. As well as leading the Fénix program[13] for the identification of the disappeared who were of interest to the police, dating back less than twenty years, Professor Lorente collaborated with the governments of Chile and Argentina to identify the "disappeared" from the dictatorships of Pinochet and Videla, respectively. At that time, the objective was to identify the seventeen guerrilla fighters of Tupac Amaro who had died after the attack on the Japanese embassy in Lima.

We exchanged several emails until Professor Lorente agreed to do DNA testing on a few of the Priaranza Thirteen. We gave him the forensic file and he selected four that he considered most identifiable if tested. The University of Granada would fund this part of the project. Mitochondrial DNA, inherited from the mothers, would be tested. Therefore, to identify the bodies, a sample would have to be taken from a sibling or from the child of a sister. In the case of Emilio Silva Faba, the DNA that could identify him would have to come from Rosa Silva, a great niece who lived in Ezpeleta, Argentina.

---

13   A highly successful collaboration between the University of Granada's Legal Medicine Department and the Guardia Civil to locate and identify persons who were "disappeared" during and after the Spanish Civil War.

After deciding who would be identified, it was determined that on March 16, Professor Lorente would go to Priaranza del Bierzo to take the samples from the remains and from the relatives. They were going to be the first victims of the Civil War to regain their identity by means of this test, and this struck us as a milestone.

$$7$$

From El Bierzo to the United Nations

T HE ROLE THAT THE Internet played in this process of the recovery of memory was crucial. Through the Web, we were able to connect with individuals and groups that helped greatly, including the International Civil Service Commission (ICSC), a non-governmental organization created between the two world wars in Zurich. This humanitarian organization had been in Spain during the Civil War, setting up food programs for children in Madrid and evacuating 6,000 children in the last months of the conflict. We found their website by chance, and after reading that they set up international workstations of all kinds, we wrote asking for their help in opening several mass graves planned for that summer.

At first, that request must have surprised them, coming from a place like Spain. Some of the ICSC's workstations dealt with the recovery of memory. One example is the workstation they set up every year at Mauthausen to restore the stairway that was built by Spanish prisoners. We had a meeting in which we laid out our objectives and set the date for the taking of samples for DNA testing of the Priaranza Thirteen. In this way, they would familiarize themselves with the terrain and have a chance to talk to some of the people who were hoping to have their relatives disinterred.

On March 15, 2002, we had dinner in Ponferrada with Professor José Antonio Lorente. During the meal, he told us that he was surprised at the young ages of the people involved in the Association for the Recovery of Historical Memory. We explained that the majority of us were grandchildren of the victims. Speaking about his university, the U of Granada, it was brought up that the most universally known of the Spanish *desaparecidos* was the poet Federico García Lorca. A few weeks later, we contacted Lorca's nephew, president of the foundation that bears his name, to see if there was any interest in searching for his remains. We thought that symbolically it would be very important, and a thorough forensic examination would shine more light on the details of his murder. But the nephew, Manuel Fernández de Montesinos, the son of the mayor of Granada who was executed at the beginning of the war, responded that he did not want to create a spectacle out of his uncle's death and that enough was already known about what happened to him.

On March 16, just after noon, Professor Lorente took samples from the four bodies selected for this procedure. The forensic report, written by the anthropologist María Encina Prada and the medical examiner Francisco Etxebarría, had explained that those were the four who presented the greatest probability for identification. Following is their report:

Individual #2. Male, 30-40 years of age and average height (5'5") whose skeleton was found face up and lying parallel to that of Individual #1. On his neck was a shoe of Individual #5. He has a strong dentition, and his upper jaw shows a missing center-right incisor, evidenced by an extension of a root which would have been attached to a dental plate. (According to information provided by the family, we know that Emilio Silva had a dental plate that was inserted in the United States.) The jaw is quite wide with an obtuse angle, giving it a squarish aspect, which corresponds to the robust jaw of Emilio Silva Faba in an archival photograph.

Due to the impacts of the bullets, the top of the head and the splanchnocranium are fractured, resulting from two shots from a firearm to the right occipital and temporal bones from back to front at an upward angle and slightly from right to left.

Individual #4. Adult male of about thirty years of age and short in stature (5' 2½" to 5' 3¾"), found lying in a prone position with his legs semi-flexed. His age is determined from the absence of degenerative structure to the vertebral column, except in the at-lantoaxial joint. The edge of the jaw is slightly squared. The lower incisors are somewhat crowded, and the dark stains on two teeth suggest a smoker. Among the objects found with this body are rubber soles of boots and pieces of woven cloth on the trunk. All of these characteristics correspond to the person of César Fernández Méndez.

The cranial fractures resulted from a projectile from a firearm penetrating the middle of the occipital bone under the inion and exiting through the face, thereby detaching part of the center portion of the frontal bone and the superciliary arches and fracturing the upper jaw at the midline of its right side. The shot follows a back to front trajectory, slightly downward and through the middle line. It may have been delivered point blank, given the loss of bone in both the internal and external cortices.

Individual #5. Young male of 20-22 years of age, no more than 25, of average height, (5' 4½"), whose body was lying face up with the arms outstretched on both sides of his torso.

Two projectiles have been recovered, one of them next to the right parietal bone, and the other in an area of the neck, of a similar caliber, corresponding to a 9 mm long. One of the shots (orifice 1) penetrates the upper region of the frontal bone, producing a radial fracture. This could have been produced by a shot at close range, based on the loss of bone in the external cortex. Orifice 3, situated on the edge of the roof of the right eye socket (orbita) corresponds to the exit of the projectile. The other shot (orifice 2) would have entered through the mid-section of the left side of the jawbone with the extraction of the internal cortex.

The exit wound, very irregular and enlarged, we found on the opposite side of the jaw, with an extraction of the external plate.

Among the objects found near this body, we found a metallic ring on the abdomen, which could have been part of the face of a watch which victim #4 probably wore, since the left hand of this person was resting on the abdomen of victim #5. Also found on the torso of this victim were pieces of fabric from articles of clothing he would have worn, in addition to some cufflinks of a good quality and shoes that could indicate that this was a person of a certain social status. These characteristics could correspond to the person of Enrique González Miguel, alias "El Madrileño" ("the man from Madrid").

Individual #13. Young adult male, approximately 25 years of age, short in stature (5' 1"), found turned slightly on his left side. His molars contain large cavities and are decayed down to the roots. His jaw contains noticeable tumors at the chin line. The cranium indicates that there was one shot to the temple, entering on the left front parietal suture and exiting through the right parietal, leaving a typical radial fracture. The presence of a lesion starting at the near edge of the right clavicle and the discovery of a projectile in the neck of the victim attest to the existence of a second shot.

In the area of the neck was found a short zipper of 4.3 inches, possibly from a sweater, and in the place that would have been the right pocket of his trousers was found a cloth-covered object that was identified as a group of coins of the era. The coins were restored by the team at the art restoration firm, Proceso Arte, headquartered in Astorga, and catalogued by Mr. Luis Grau of the Museum of León. The five coins included: a silver peseta from the Provisional Government (1869); two 5-cent bronze coins from the Provisional Government (1868-1874); a 25-cent coin of the Second Republic (1931-1939); and a 20-real bronze coin minted in Portugal under Luis I (1884). On the soles of the shoes, in good condition, there was still visible a chariot, the mark of the Venus brand of shoes. These characteristics correspond to the person of Juan Francisco Falagán.

In the hall were several family members, among them Francisco Falagán, a man of 85 years, possibly the brother of victim #13, who had lost yet another brother in the war. At first, Francisco did not want to be noticed during the process of taking the samples; he was fearful. But when he saw the remains of what could have been his brother on the table, he stood up, visibly shaken, and allowed Professor Lorente to take a blood sample in the presence of several journalists and relatives.

That afternoon, we went with several members of the ICSC to the mass gravesite at Fresnedo, where Vicente Moreira's mother's remains had been found along with those of three men. Accompanying us was Isabel González Losada, the 83-year-old woman who was searching for the body of her brother Eduardo, which had been found in an unmarked grave at the entrance to Piedrafita de Babia. Isabel had witnessed the exhumation at Priaranza and she had sent us a notarized affidavit that she had drawn up with a friend of hers, Asunción Álvarez, who had a similar story. Together they had gone to the office of a senior attorney, accompanied by two witnesses, where they revealed everything they knew about the deaths of their brothers, in the expectation that this would be converted into a public document; in the event of their deaths, this information would be available to someone wishing to disinter the bodies.

On Sunday, March 22, 2002, the day after the DNA samples were taken, the national newspaper *El Mundo* opened its Sunday special section with a report entitled, "Opening the Mass Graves of Francoism." In the article was an account of the work we had thus far completed, as well as our email address and web page.

During the last week of March, we studied the web page of the United Nations High Commissioner for Human Rights. The attorney, Elena Reviriego, had been researching the Spanish *desaparecidos* for months. She had compiled the laws that the self-imposed Franco government had promulgated and executed after the end of the war through which it helped the families of "those who died for God and for Spain" find their remains, exhume them, and transfer them to their hometowns. Her plan was to expose as a historical injustice the fact that some families had received official State help and others had received none, even with the arrival of democracy. She spoke with us about the possibility of appealing to the United Nations to help us with our cause.

On the High Commissioner for Human Rights' web page, we found Resolution 47/133, the "Declaration On the Protection of All Persons From Enforced Disappearance," which had been approved by the General Assembly on December 18, 1992 (Appendix I). As we read it, we could not believe how aligned it was with our objectives—resulting, as it had been, from international pressure after the cases of "disappearance" during the dictatorships in Argentina and Chile—and it opened for us the possibility of initiating a demand before the High Commissioner that the UN pressure the Spanish government to begin a widespread search for the "disappeared."

The reading of that text filled us with hope, because it revealed the existence of a way to demand help for the families. Though it seemed somewhat outside of the realm of possibilities, after numerous calls to the High Commissioner, we managed to contact Tamara Kunanayakam, Secretary of the Working Group on Enforced and Involuntary Disappearances. We described for her the work the ARMH had done thus far and the goals we had reached. We asked her some questions that relatives of victims had asked us to communicate to her. Her answer to every question, to our amazement, was "yes." She told us that the families had recourse to demand the remains from the battlefronts; in a war between nations, that was the purview of the International Red Cross, but in a civil war, assuming that the winning side would hide information, families of victims had the power to demand the remains of their relatives who had fallen in combat.

Tamara Kunananyakam invited us to attend the next meeting of the Working Group on Enforced Disappearances in New York in mid-August. The UN has a form that relatives must complete, providing information on the circumstances of the disappearance and the identity of the victim. Although the form requires a lot of information, it is merely a point of departure for the investigation:

a. Complete name of the "disappeared" person, as well as all other information pertinent to his or her identification, e.g., national I.D. number, photograph, etc.

b. Month, day and year of disappearance.

c. Place of arrest or abduction, or where the disappeared person was last seen.

d. Ideas about who could have carried out the abduction or arrest.

e. Information on any methods used by relatives or others to locate the disappeared person, e.g., questions posed to authorities, requests for habeas corpus, etc.

f. Identity of the person or organization making the request (name and address, which will be held confidential).

8
One Large Mass Grave Named Spain

ON APRIL 1, 2002, the anniversary of the end of the Civil War, a couple of my closest associates and I were invited to appear on the radio program *Hoy por hoy* on *Cadena SER*.[14] The journalist Iñaki Gabilondo interviewed us with regard to the ARMH, the kind of people we were searching for, and the significance of an exhumation in towns where the topic of the Civil War continued to be a taboo in spite of Spain's last twenty-five years of democracy. Starting that day, more people began contacting us.

About two weeks later, and after speaking with the High Commissioner, we established the need to present at least twenty-five cases to be able to give a certain weight to our demands. On the radio program *Hoy por hoy*, we announced the need to count among those interested in our cause at least twenty-five family members of people who "disappeared" during the Civil War and its aftermath. We thought about demanding the remains of the poet Federico García Lorca, something to which we had a right. Even his biographer, Ian Gibson, was willing to fill out the paperwork. However, we desisted, because more than anything, we were determined to respect the wishes of the families.

Two days after making that announcement on the program, we were contacted by seventy-five families willing to cooperate with us. We had a deadline of August 5 to present our case in Geneva and secure a place on the agenda of the Working Group's meeting in New York. Around that same time, we met Montserrat Sans, an attorney,

---

14 *Hoy por hoy* is the most popular news program on Spanish radio. *Cadena SER* is Spain's premier radio network.

the granddaughter of Catalan *republicanos* exiled in France, who had worked for several years in the UN on issues related to enforced disappearances. "Montse" helped orient us as to the steps we needed to take and offered to present our case in New York. She lived in Washington and had abundant experience in international law and human rights. She was probably the best person we could have met for our purposes.

Soon after beginning our work on the exhumations, we thought about the possibility of suing to have the State take over the disinterments and identifications. We did not realize to what extent we had been influenced by the Pinochet case, which had opened the possibility of having something similar occur in Spain. The attorney who was working with us, Elena Reviriego, had had a connection with the Pinochet matter and also worked on the mass grave cases in Guatemala which were dealt with in the National High Court in Madrid.

Due to the UN resolution and the bearing it had on the the families of the *republicanos* killed in the war and the postwar period, as well as Franco's refusal to honor the Geneva Convention of 1930, Elena Reviriego began to prepare the lawsuit that would allow us to petition the Justice system to open the graves and identify the bodies.

The UN resolution is still not a standard and therefore is not part of the laws judges are required to enforce. But it was a norm on which the judicial power could lean to open records, begin an investigation and look for those "disappeared" persons. I recall that around that time the Argentine newspaper *La Nación* interviewed us. The article began with a critique of Spanish Judge Baltazar Garzón of the High Court, saying that "the shoemaker's son always goes barefoot." The reporter spent the first paragraph explaining that in the country of the judge who had begun the process of searching for the *desaparecidos* in Chile and Argentina, there was a marked silence about the history of thousands of men and women whose families knew nothing about their fate, in many cases, since the Francoist military uprising in 1936. On many occasions, the foreign press has asked us about Baltazar Garzón's attitude toward the Spanish *desaparecidos*, and our answer has remained the same: "judicial silence."

In May 2002, we began preparations for an international work group in which several people from different countries were going to collaborate with us on the opening of common graves. We had to find accommodations for them, as well as cooking facilities. The work was going to take two weeks and we would open five unmarked graves. The first week, the volunteers and the group of archaeologists stayed in Piedrafita de Babia and the second week in Cubillos del Sil.

In conversations with the ICSC, we thought of two options for selecting the work group dates: the second half of June or the first half of July. We strategically went with the second option which proved more fruitful for our group's publicity in the media, since on June 30 the World Cup ended and the Spanish presidency of the European Union came to an end, and there was space in the press for other types of news.

Working with the media was intense. We inserted into our email list 372 foreign and domestic news outlets whom we contacted periodically, updating them on our progress. Some left-leaning entities criticized us then for being too media-conscious, but from the beginning we knew that we had to use the media to break the silence about that period in our history, to reach the maximum number of people possible, and to open a debate in Spanish society about the consequences of Francoism.

In June, the first volunteers began appearing at the work group site. We had established that twelve participants would collaborate with the archaeologists in all the tasks that were deemed necessary. We also wanted them to visit the neighboring towns and to talk with the residents about the Spanish Civil War so that they would hear firsthand about that part of our history. The final list consisted of three Spaniards, including the coordinator of the group; a Czech man; a Polish woman; a Dutch woman; two Americans; a Frenchman residing in Israel; a French woman, granddaughter of a Spanish exile at the end of the war; an Italian, grandson of a member of the Garibaldi International Brigade; a Dutch student of History; a Polish woman who had lost several relatives at Auschwitz; an Austrian student of Social Anthropology; and a seventy-two year old Swiss woman who had come to honor her two best friends, Spanish exiles in Paris who had been tortured in prison in Segovia and died in exile.

We would also include Mari Luz González, one of the archaeologists who had participated in the exhumations in Priaranza and
Fresnedo, and four other archaeologists, members of the Aranzadi Society of Sciences. The volunteers would stay the first week in a house
provided by the government of Cabrillanes de Babia. They would sleep
in sleeping bags on mats, prepare their own meals, and share the only
bathroom in the house. For the archaeologists, we had reserved a hos-
tel which would provide meals and which would also accommodate
some members of the ARMH, in addition to Theo Francos, a French
member of the International Brigade who was of Spanish origin and
whom we invited to spend two or three days at the worksite, though
he ended up spending two weeks with us.

The Association had almost no funds, so part of the expenses in-
curred at the worksite were paid from our personal funds. The government of Cabrillanes de Babia could not pay the living expenses of the
group, so each day the volunteers would make a shopping list that we
would take to the shops in town. Town officials would ask the two
bakers to take turns delivering bread to the residence of the volunteers.

For the second week of the work, the government of Cubillos del
Sil would lend us a center and would open an account in one of the
stores where the volunteers would be able to purchase provisions freely. The ICSC was very careful when it came to expenses, and the daily
food allotment was one euro (just over $1) per person.

9
No More Forgetting

ON THE MORNING OF July 1, 2002, the first volunteers began arriving in Cabrillanes de Babia. I drove there earlier that day, accompanied by the volunteers from Switzerland and Poland. I left them in the house they would be staying in and then went over to city hall to prepare the final details of the project.

That day, something occurred in the press that changed our whole media profile. In the national newspaper *El País* there appeared a page written by the reporter Carlos E. Cué, entitled "The Earth Returns Its Dead." During the drive toward the area of Babia my telephone rang incessantly. It was a sign of what was to come in the next days. We think that Cué's article marked the turning point in the diffusion of our work and somehow made it politically correct. Later we learned that until that moment it had been the most-read page in the history of *El País Digital*, with 53,000 visitors.

Throughout the day the rest of the volunteers arrived, and we reviewed a few details so that everything would be ready. We purchased food, prepared the sleeping area, and while everyone was getting acquainted, we located the materials we would need for the excavation. That same day there arrived in El Bierzo a georadar, a machine that could detect changes in density in the subsoil. We used this device to locate and mark the common graves, to facilitate the archaeologists' work, and to save on the time we would need for the excavators which were provided by the local governments who were collaborating with us. That same machine had been used in Bolivia to locate the remains of Che Guevara. In our case, however, it was a failed experiment. We wanted to test the possibilities of its use, and we managed to do so thanks to the government of Villablino, which collaborated with us generously by paying the bill from the company that transported the machine from Valencia. Unfortunately, the use of that technology was of little benefit, possibly because normally it is used in Spain to search for minerals, and there are no personnel trained in the detection of organic remains. If the results had been more favorable, it would have been an especially useful tool for future excavations.

In the afternoon, we went with a group of volunteers and archaeologists to the farm where the unmarked grave was located, in Piedrafita de Babia. We examined the terrain to determine where exactly to excavate. Suddenly a man came up to us and indicated where there was another mass grave. He said that when he was digging a hole on his land to plant a tree, underneath some thick grass he came across a human bone. Pushing the grass aside, he saw that he was at a gravesite that had been marked with stones. The region of Babia had been an area of retreat when, in October of 1937, Asturias fell to the Nationalists. The Francoist forces arrested many people trying to escape and executed them there, leaving common graves all over the region.

On the morning of Tuesday, July 2, volunteers, archaeologists and members of the Association arrived at the site of the excavation, where the last exploration with the georadar had just begun. The technicians who were using the machine marked the area where we would find the grave with little flags. In the marked-off area, the manual work began with picks and shovels. All morning the buckets of dirt yielded nothing to indicate we were at the right spot. It was thought that the remains of thirty-seven people would be found there, although that number could have been different.

Around mid-morning, Isabel González and Asunción Álvarez arrived. It was an emotional moment when we introduced the volunteers who had come to lend a hand and said what countries they had come from. Their arrival moved all of us who were there, especially when Asunción, a very religious woman, said to us, her voice choked with emotion, "May the Lord keep all obstacles from your path." Isabel and Asunción spoke for a few minutes with each of them and thanked them immensely for the work they were doing, and I think this was the first time they really understood the importance that this international effort held for the families.

During those first hours, the residents of the area approached the site to offer any pertinent information they had. We had a sketch that Asunción Álvarez had drawn years earlier, though we opted not to use it, preferring instead to follow the indications of the georadar. By late morning the archaeologists decided that we needed an excavator to find the remains, since the farm on which we were searching was over 8600 square feet, thus impossible to excavate manually. The government of Villablino loaned us their excavator, which at 4:00 p.m. sharp began making trenches systematically at more than six and one-half feet deep and spaced almost five feet apart.

The area residents continued pointing out different spots on the farm. One man in particular stood in front of the bucket of the excavator until the operator heeded his request to have a certain place examined, and they went to where there was a small hill. For the archaeologists this was a little delicate, since they knew it was better to do a systematic search, but they also realized that perhaps one of those testimonies could help them find the remains sooner rather than later. That afternoon yielded no results, something that had become fairly standard for us, given our prior excavations.

The next morning, the excavator continued digging up the dirt without anything of interest appearing. Discouragement finally reared its ugly head among the workers. By then, the site was full of news media and our phones were ringing constantly. Families who were looking for "disappeared" relatives were calling from all parts of Spain, and Spanish and foreign news media were wanting to interview relatives of the fallen. All the national television stations were represented, in addition to TVE *Informe Semanal* (a Spanish television program on current events, including cultural topics and sports), the German channel *ZDF*, and photographers from major news agencies such as Reuters and the Associated Press.

The less land there remained to excavate, the higher the tension rose. There was still the possibility that the remains had dissolved if the land were very acidic and damp, or if they had been buried under the asphalt of the widened highway. Finally, by midday, we were going to excavate the place Asunción Álvarez had drawn years before, a copy of which she had given to Isabel.

That afternoon the work resumed in the midst of great consternation; there remained little land left to search, and if nothing appeared, the frustration, especially for the families, would be palpable. At 5:35 p.m., however, when only a few square meters of that farm were left untouched, after which the work on that farm would be definitively finished, we discovered a femur.

At that moment, Isabel and Asunción happened to be in a neighboring town, Vega de Viejos, speaking with a woman of their age, who was telling them about the Civil War in that region and who, years before, had given the two women useful information about it. Someone from our group got word to Isabel and Asunción that some remains of the victims had finally appeared at the grave, and when the two women arrived at the site, all of us became emotional. They had waited sixty-five years, and time had given them the ability to live this moment. Stepping close to the grave, Isabel said, "I hope to see the remains of my brother, even if all I see are bones."

Isabel recounted that her brother, Eduardo, had enlisted in the *republicano* militia and had participated in the defense of Asturias. In October of 1937, when the Nationalist rebels took control of the area, he met up with a group of friends outside his hometown, Palacios del Sil. The seven men stayed in the mountains, not daring to return home for fear of reprisals for having defended the Republic. Eduardo and Isabel's father appealed to their local government and was told that if the seven men would surrender, nothing would happen to them; they simply had to stop by the government offices and would be granted amnesty. After considerable discussion, because some of the men did not trust the officials, they decided to turn themselves in. Once they arrived at the government offices, they were arrested and taken to the military headquarters in Villablino where, in the wee hours of November 6, 1937, they were removed and taken toward the detention center of San Marcos in León. But on arriving in Piedrafita de Babia the seven were executed on the side of the road.

The stories of people who were executed affect the townspeople, as well. One of the residents most affected when the remains appeared in the excavation at Piedrafita de Babia was Ricardo Suárez. One after-noon when he was still a child, Ricardo was walking with his mother toward a meadow on their land when their dog pulled away from the road and ran into the brush, sniffing and barking. Ricardo followed him and discovered a large pool of blood on recently disturbed earth. At the time, Ricardo had two brothers who had escaped and were hid-ing in the mountains, and he thought the unmarked grave could con-tain their corpses. He said nothing to his mother at the time, fearing that she would come to the same conclusion. But three days later he could not contain himself any longer, and he told her of his discovery. From that day on, the mother and son would go each day to cry at the gravesite. But one month later, they had news from the brothers, and their anguish turned to joy. Still, Ricardo would always remember that grave as something tragic, and when the excavator unearthed the first bones, Ricardo burst into tears.

The townspeople would not dare to properly bury the bodies of victims out of fear of reprisals. The priest of Piedrafita said in one ser-mon something unforgettable: "How terrible those men must have been if even the earth does not want them!" Finally, a group of resi-dents of the town got together and decided to cover the bodies with cartfuls of dirt to keep the vermin from prowling around the area—an act of bravery since, if caught, they could have met with serious trou-ble from the Falangists of the region.

The evening the remains were discovered, some of the dirt was pushed aside and the excavation was interrupted until the next morn-ing. Before dinner, we had a meeting with the international volunteers to tell them they should divide into two groups. In the morning, one group would go to Villablino to talk with the older people and com-pile data on the Civil War, to try to locate more unmarked graves, and to record first-person stories from those years. The other group would excavate with the archaeologists, and in the afternoon they would switch places.

Some weeks before the excavation began, we wrote letters to the embassies of Germany and Italy, inviting them to attend one of the exhumations to acknowledge the suffering of families during the war, and as a sign of atonement for the two countries' close collaboration with General Francisco Franco after his sedition. We had no response from the Italian embassy, but the Germans sent us a letter signed by Udo Volz, a protocol officer, dated July 3, 2002. Following is the content of the letter:

Dear Sirs:

Thank you so much for your letter of June 22, 2002, addressed to Ambassador Joachim Bitterlich, in which you invite the Embassy to attend an act of exhumation of victims of the Civil War which will be held in León in early July.

I understand that your invitation is tied to the review of one of the most notorious chapters of Spanish history of the twentieth century, in which, in a principal way, and along with other European countries, Germany is implicated.

Fortunately, Spain and Germany today are strong democracies that work shoulder to shoulder to help our European Community thrive.

This must not allow us to forget our history, not at all. Recently, there was a commemoration of the anniversary of the bombing of Guernica, with a solemn ceremony in the cemetery there, with German participation.

Nevertheless, if this Embassy does not wish to take part in the exhumation, it is due to not wanting this to be a sign of any misinterpretation. Though you may feel disappointed at this decision, I beg you not to consider it as any disparagement of the victims of the Spanish Civil War.

This was not the first time we had requested that symbolic gesture. In October of 2000, when we were about to open the grave at Priaranza, we had sent similar letters, and on that occasion the response from the German embassy contained a joke in very poor taste: a drawing of a skull and an airplane which supposedly an embassy employee had included in the letter, thereby changing the meaning of the text. We asked for an explanation, as those symbols could not have been included by accident, given Germany's participation in the Spanish

Civil War. Consul Radkle called us to a meeting with an interpreter and a computer specialist from the embassy. There they explained to us that the problem had been the word processor of our computer. We said we used the same word processor as 98% of Europeans and we doubted the German embassy would send those drawings far and wide. On revealing our suspicion that someone had sent the drawings intentionally, the interpreter started laughing at us, at which point we ended the meeting. I recall that a few weeks after the attacks on the twin towers in New York in 2003, some newspapers published a notice that in official centers they were receiving written documents in which there appeared a tower and an airplane, ostensibly the result of a "word processing glitch."

The repercussion that the excavation in Piedrafita de Babia had in the media was something unexpected, in spite of our having worked for several months to break the silence surrounding that part of our history. A few months earlier we had interviewed the French sociologist Alain Touraine, who had studied the transitions to democracy in Latin America. I told him about our excavation of the grave in Priaranza and the resistance that existed in Spain to deal with those topics, as if before the transition we had not had a dictatorship. Touraine commented that in Germany and in France, where they had collaborated with Nazism, they had needed about twenty-five years to seriously come to terms with that part of their history, and that it was a process that would unfold naturally.

The gravesite at Piedrafita de Babia was located six kilometers from Somiedo, in an area where many Asturians had died. Over the days of our excavation work there, dozens of Asturians stopped by to talk with us or simply to ask for our phone number. Our impact on the Asturian region was substantial; almost daily over the course of two months, the press there published informative articles dealing with the topic of the "disappeared." I remember one old couple—over 80 years old—approaching the gravesite on foot and with difficulty from where they had parked their car. When they came close, they asked for me by name, and when I walked over to them the woman said that they were from a town near Oviedo. She took a piece of paper out of her pocket and explained that what she was holding was the last letter that her brother had written from Vega de Viejos, a town 6 kilometers from Piedrafita. The woman read me the letter and when she finished, she thanked me. Walking away, I overheard her say to her husband, "It was about time someone paid attention to us."

Hearing that made me angry. During the transition to democracy, Spanish society left behind thousands of families who had favored the *Republicano* cause, families who had been considered "anti-Spanish," the same families who had put aside their legitimate protests so that the transition process could be smooth. But by the year 2002, it was no longer possible to closet the truth. It was one thing to have a political debate about whether collective amnesty was necessary or not, but it was another to see the faces and hear the lives of those victims' families and not try to do something to help them.

On the night of July 6, the television program *Informe Semanal* ("Weekly Report") had a segment on the excavation. All of those who had participated in the work, as well as some who had come to offer support, met in a bar to watch the show. We were interested to see how they would portray this subject on one of the most important programs of public television's information services. The journalist Ana Bosch did an impressive job that felt to us like a small victory. This was a good step in the direction of public reparation for all the families who had suffered in silence the erasure of their loved ones and of themselves, and the sadness of living in a democracy that did not remember the men and women who first opened Spain's doors to it.

10
Toward Historical Justice

ON SUNDAY, JULY 7, the work at the excavation site ended. The following morning the archaeologists would raise the remains from out of the ground and we would then head for Cubillos del Sil where we would open several more unmarked graves. One of our objectives was to see the justice system take over the investigation and identification of the bodies. That morning we phoned the examining magistrate of Villablino, who was on duty, and after several attempts I managed to reach her cell phone. Several days earlier I had had to appear at the headquarters of the Civil Guard of Villablino to give a statement on the excavation in Piedrafita. As I had the right to present my case, I submitted the UN Resolution on Enforced and Involuntary Disappearance and maintained that I wanted the judge to apply this resolution to our work in Piedrafita and to try to identify the seven bodies that had been found there.

Our goal was to have the judge attend the retrieval of the bodies, thus establishing a precedent. But she rejected our offer, saying that the judicial police were preparing a report for her and that that was as much contact as she wanted with the case. Nevertheless, she did agree to see me the next morning in her office.

That same morning, we published a press release, and Channel SER opened one of its news broadcasts with the announcement that the judge in Villablino had refused to appear at the recently opened unmarked grave. Our relationship with the media had changed remarkably; prior to setting up the work site, our press releases would end up in the black hole of unpublished information, but now the media were attentive; we had a nice collection of media sources and journalists who would receive our press releases in a matter of minutes.

That Sunday evening, after a week that was so busy that we never stopped working, I sat on a rock at the edge of the grave and lived what for me was a moment of profound meaning. Isabel González was at one edge of the excavation site. Several family members and residents had come there to see her. Isabel welcomed them, they asked her how it was going, and then they would peer into the grave to contemplate the remains of the seven men. At that moment it dawned on me how important those excavations were to the families, because they could now begin to prepare funeral services that were more than sixty years in limbo, and they could prepare to grieve—a rite so essential for people who have grown up in a funerary culture such as ours.

Then, I looked to my right and saw Ricardo Suárez who, as a boy, came across that pool of blood on the ground. Now, more than eighty years old, he was surrounded by five young men and women to whom he was telling about those terribly difficult years of the Civil War. At that moment I realized that those two scenes symbolized the two fundamental objectives that our Association needed to have: first, to allow the families the opportunity to recover their dignity by giving a proper burial to their relatives; and secondly, that the old could relate to the next generations their testimony so that they could take possession of the history that was kept from them due to Spain's continued silence during the transition to democracy.

Emilio Silva Faba, civilian victim of the Fascist repression at the start of the Spanish Civil War and grandfather of the author. (Photo courtesy of Emilio Silva Barrera)

Exhumation in October 2000 of the Priaranza Thirteen, the first mass grave opened using scientific methods to identify victims of the Franco repression. (Photo courtesy of Emilio Silva Barrera)

Residents of the area around Priaranza gather daily to observe the excavation of the unmarked mass grave, having known of its existence since childhood. (Photo courtesy of Emilio Silva Barrera)

Emilio, Ramón and Manuel Silva Santín at their father's gravesite in October, 2000. (Photo courtesy of Emilio Silva Barrera)

Emilio Silva Barrera, speaking on the tenth anniversary of the exhumation of the Priaranza Thirteen, when a plaque to commemorate them was placed at the site of their unmarked common grave. (Photo courtesy of Emilio Silva Barrera)

Commemorative plaque at the roadside grave of the Priaranza Thirteen. (Photo courtesy of Emilio Silva Barrera)

On Monday morning I went to the judge's office in Villablino. The judge received me warmly. I had spoken with our lawyer, Elena Reviriego, who had advised me not to argue the legality of the matter, but to focus on the human aspect. I was told that an examining magistrate can open records and request all types of tests. To that end, I told her that I had spent a year and a half arranging for DNA tests on some of the remains that were discovered in my grandfather's grave, but in the case of Piedrafita de Babia, two women of eighty-four and eighty-seven years of age who were waiting for results possibly would not be able to wait long to identify their brothers.

Upon leaving the judge's office I went to pick up a few things from the store, and when I arrived at the excavation site, I ran into the members of the judicial police who were taking a statement from the archaeologist Mari Luz González and the forensic anthropologist María Encina Prada. One of the members of the Civil Guard informed me that the judge had opened records and that DNA tests would probably be done. We had managed to set an important precedent which we might use again in future cases. We decided then to save for another occasion the petition that Elena Reviriego had drawn up and which I had taken with me for Isabel González' signature.

The remains were exhumed and deposited in a building owned by the government of Cabrillanes, which was declared the judicial depository. There they were subjected to forensic analysis. In total, there were seven bodies, not thirty-seven as had been claimed at one point. We did not learn what happened to the others. However, near Piedrafita is the bridge of the Palomas, and from its more than 80-meter height, prisoners were thrown down to the rocks of the Babia River. Sometimes the prisoners were already dead, and they would be taken from a trailer and tossed into the abyss.

We arrived in Cubillos del Sil in the wee hours of the morning. Some members of the Association were waiting for us in the social hall of the government building, with a meal prepared. We were exhausted and slept soundly thereafter. Hours later, we would divide into two groups: one would excavate in Cabañinas where there were two known unmarked graves with two and three bodies, and the other would leave each morning for San Pedro de Olleros where they would exhume two bodies. In Cabañinas we lived some of the most dramatic moments of our lives.

Senén's eyes were scouring the land, as if in search of a piece of his childhood that one day the Falangists had snatched from him. The archaeologists had spent two days recovering the remains of his father, his uncle, and three other men. The hours and minutes of that day in which their biography was cut short are clearly engraved in his memory. "It was Tuesday, it was Tuesday," he repeated, arms leaning on the scaffolding and eyes fixed on that hole in the ground that had swallowed his childhood. It was the morning of September 1, 1936. "They took five hours to destroy our lives." Summoned by the local priest, the Falangists began looking for weapons. "They searched the town and when they came up with nothing they took my father, my uncle, and three other men from town. They put them in a truck and took off." Senén ran after them trying to rescue his father from certain death. He ran and ran until he no longer could. "They took him; they took him from us to kill him here and punish his whole family."

Senén García dedicated his life to working the mine and cultivating some of his family's farmlands. For many decades he did not speak with anyone about the place where his father's remains rested. It was a secret that was whispered in dark kitchens or bedrooms. Only five years ago his daughter Rosa discovered where her grandfather had died. "No one ever told me that they had buried him in a grave along a road I travel almost every day."

Near kilometer 11 of the road that goes from Ponferrada toward Villablino there were two unmarked graves containing the bodies of five men: brothers Pascual and Antonio García, Florentino Enríquez, Santiago García Arroyo, and Cesáreo Fernández. These last three were residents of Fresnedo. All five were murdered that first day of September after leaving Fresnedo in that truck Senén could not catch.

The race toward his departing father was not the end of the tragedy, as on the way back to his town he saw billowing smoke. His house and that of his uncle were on fire. Running toward his house, he saw a group of Falangists eating the cured ham that only hours before had been hanging in his family's kitchen. "Go console your mother," they said to him.

With the excavation of the grave, Senén was finally able to catch up with the truck that had taken his father from him, and he saw him dead for the first time. Fear is still the order of the day with these people who, despite living under democracy, have not seen any guarantee that they can speak freely.

The same day his father's grave was opened, Senén García still maintained that he really did not know if recovering his remains was worth the trouble. Up to the last moment, he resisted looking at the evidence of what had happened to his father after he was taken away by force in the Falangists' truck. But when the archaeologists found the first human remains, he began living the grief that for years he had kept bottled up inside. Senén walked close to one of the archaeologists and asked that the bones be handled gently. From time to time, he would ask something or make a comment, or murmur "Why did they have to burn down our house?" He was remembering everything his mother endured.

The excavation in Cabañinas was complicated. The location of the two graves had been indicated by relatives who had made a clandestine cemetery behind some bushes. Next to one of the graves was a piece of slate on which a son of one of the murdered men had carved with a knife the dates he spent time at that spot when he visited his hometown from Argentina.

Today one can see a monument where the two graves had been, erected in memory of those five men. Two large slabs of slate were embedded into the hole that had served as the graves, and next to them were planted five olive trees as a historic symbol. The day before the dedication of the monument, the five men had been buried in the cemetery of Fresnedo, where their families could pay their respects.

The group of international volunteers finished their labors on July 13, 2002. That night the government of Cubillos del Sil offered a farewell dinner for all those of us who had worked on the exhumation of the graves. It was a truly special event. The volunteers spoke about how much that experience had affected them. The International Brigade member Theo Francos assured everyone that he had thoroughly enjoyed sharing that time with the young people who were determined not to let that part of our history fall into a black hole. The mayor of Cubillos, José Luis Ramón, said that the doors to the town were wide open for us anytime we wished to return. The next day, the governing board of El Bierzo invited the volunteers on a tour of the region so they could see some of the most noteworthy sights in El Bierzo.

For the members of the Association, that work group was seen as a total success. Not only did we help several families, but we also elicited from them discussion about the "disappeared" *republicanos* from the Civil War. Our phones never stopped ringing those days, and every step we took resulted in more work, as many more families than we expected appeared at the worksites and revealed that they had relatives who were thought to have been murdered. However, our means were limited; the core of our group amounted to five members, and we were already overburdened.

On July 16 we received a call from the Parliamentary Group of Izquierda Unida (United Left political party), saying that they were going to raise an issue that very day in a session of Congress about the unmarked graves so that the government would have to take a stand on the matter. The text of their question follows:

To the Executive Committee of the House of Representatives

In accordance with the rules of the House of Representatives, we present this question to the Government in expectation of a written response. Thanks to the work that the Association for the Recovery of Historical Memory has been doing since the year 2000, there have been exhumed the remains of some of the "disappeared" and executed anti-Francoist fighters during the Civil War and the postwar period, buried in a common grave in Piedrafita de Babia. With the excavations that the Association is carrying out, it will be possible to identify those remains and return them to their families so that finally, after 60 years, they may have a decent burial.

Since this excavation began, hundreds of people from all parts of Spain have been in touch with the Association to ask for its help in the search for their relatives who disappeared during the Civil War. It is thought that more than 35,000 people, murdered by the Nationalist forces, remain buried in mass graves. Once the Civil War ended, the Franco dictatorship funded the exhumation and relocation of the bodies of its forces (an order from May 1, 1940 spoke of the "just hopes of the families of those who gloriously died for God and for Spain, victims of the red brutality" and "with relatives murdered by the Marxist hordes"). Now, after 40 years of dictatorship and 25 of democracy, we are trying to return their identity to those men and women who were murdered and "disappeared" for defending a legitimately established order and who deserve public recognition from Spanish society.

To that end, the Spanish Government should set in motion all the means necessary for the location and excavation of all the unmarked graves in Spanish territory; identify the remains of those people and return to their families said remains. In this way we will rescue from oblivion the thousands of "disappeared" and dignity will be restored to their memory and their families.

With this in mind, we ask the following questions:

Is the Government aware of the work being done by the Association for the Recovery of Historical Memory?

Does the Government know its obligation to investigate the "disappeared" persons from the Civil War, which is upheld by a 1992 resolution by the General Assembly of the United Nations regarding enforced and permanent disappearances?

Has the Government seen to the availability of the means necessary to locate and exhume from the unmarked graves the remains of those who were "disappeared" and executed by the Franco forces during the Civil War, so that they may be identified?

Does the State, in particular the Ministry of Defense, have the technology capable of detecting human remains under the ground so that the location of the common graves is more accurate?

We were told by the United Left that the Government had thirty days to reply to their questions. The response would be crucial for us because it would be binding, and it would reveal to us the willingness of the Partido Popular to apply the UN resolution. The Government's response took three months to arrive, and it did not shed any light on the problem at hand.

Response

The Department of the Interior is aware that from July 2-8, 2002, the Association for the Recovery of Historical Memory conducted a search in the third parcel of area 21 of the municipality of Cabrillanes (León), in Piedrafita de Babia, for a common grave containing human remains from the Spanish Civil War.

This grave contained the remains of seven people that are now in the cemetery of Villablino (León) under the auspices of the judge of the trial court of said location and under the protection of the Judicial Police and Civil Guard of Villablino.

With regard to subsequent activities of this nature, we are awaiting resolutions which are forthcoming from the judicial authority. Finally, the Director of the Department of the Interior has available forensic anthropological services to identify the bones, using DNA testing, but resources to detect these remains in the subsoil are limited.

Right around that time, a debate on the state of the nation was taking place. Members of the opposition, including Iñaki Anasagasti of the Basque Nationalist Party (PNV), and Gaspar Llamazares of Izquierda Unida (United Left) made reference to the "disappeared" in the unmarked graves. The response from the President of the Government, José María Aznar, was that we should leave the ghosts of the past in the past, because Spaniards wanted to look toward the future, which seemed contradictory given the hundreds of families who had called us asking for help.

11
The "Disappeared" Spaniards at the United Nations

AFTER THE INTERNATIONAL GROUP of volunteers dispersed, we had to get busy working with the UN. We had received dozens of applications, but many were not filled out completely. In general, this was due to a lack of information or fear on the part of the families about completing the form. On August 5 we had to submit them in Geneva so that from there, on the 14th, the officials on the Enforced Disappearance Working Group could take them to New York.

We studied the cases we had received and selected a total of 64 that had the minimum requirements for any possible further investigation. One week earlier, we learned that the families had to have presented a document before a Spanish government entity. To resolve this, we registered the 64 files with the Office of the Ombudsman, thus fulfilling that obligation for acceptance by the UN task force.

On August 5, after three days driving with my wife and three children, I arrived at Wilson Palace, the headquarters of the office of the UN High Commissioner for Human Rights in Geneva. I was carrying two folders, one with photocopies of the files and documents submitted by the families, and the other containing summaries of the files in English and Spanish to facilitate the work of the UN employees so that the maximum number of cases could be debated in New York.

I laid out for Tamara Kunanayakam, the secretary of the Working Group on the "disappeared," how the Association had been created, from the opening of the grave in Priaranza to the recent international volunteer work group. After answering her questions and handing her the folders with the documentation, we went to another room which was equipped for audiovisual presentations so that she could see a video of the July 6th segment of *Weekly Report*.

As she was listening to the report on the excavation in Piedrafita de Babia, and as Isabel and Asunción related their families' tragic histories, Tamara was visibly moved. I tried to read signs of hope in each one of her gestures, the possibility of our case being accepted and the subsequent opening of an investigation in Spain into the whereabouts of all the men and women whose families had not received any word of their death. On finishing the viewing of the video, there was discussion about having it seen by members of the task force who would be meeting in New York. I gave her the tape that I had brought so that it could be seen by Isabel Eiriz, a Spanish psychologist specializing in treating victims of political violence, who had sent us an email from her home in Lausanne.

On August 11, 2002, *El País Semanal* (the national newspaper *El País'* Week in Review) published a report on the international work group, written by the journalist Rodolfo Serrano. Beginning that day, our email started overflowing, and we had to open a new address with more megabytes of memory to store all the information we were receiving. Dozens of families wrote to us that month asking to become members of the Association and also asking for forms to fill out regarding their "disappeared" relatives, which they then sent to a post office box in Ponferrada.

For the report in *El País Week In Review*, they had asked me for a short text, which I titled "The Time for Memory":

> I took years to realize that my grandfather was a *desaparecido*. His name was Emilio Silva Faba. I never heard my grandmother speak of him, but as a child I would hear things from others: that he had served with the Rebublican Left, that on October 16, 1936, he had been summoned to the government headquarters in Villafranca del Bierzo and that he had been arrested. That same night they killed him along with twelve other men. The thirteen bodies were left buried in a roadside ditch at the entrance to Priaranza.

Sixty-four years later, I went to find him. As I researched the place where his grave was to be found, an old man told me ironically that there were more dead outside the cemetery than inside. Thanks to the selfless assistance of many people, on October 28, 2000, we succeeded in exhuming the thirteen bodies. A group of archaeologists, forensic anthropologists and others who simply wanted to be in solidarity with us made possible the exhumation of the individual victims. In those days, many people with "disappeared" relatives came to see us and ask us for help. To that end, we created the Association for the Recovery of Historical Memory and discovered that this was an issue that affected thousands of Spaniards.

If all goes well, my grandfather will be identified, thanks to the University of Granada and DNA testing. We will finally be able to bury him next to my grandmother, Modesta, who cried over his death for sixty years. By then we will have made known to the UN High Commissioner for Human Rights the forced disappearance of 300 people from the Civil War and its aftermath. Their families await the moment when History will do justice to these people, and they can give them a proper burial. Our goal is that the State take responsibility for the exhumations and identifications. Those "grandfathers" are the fathers and mothers of our democracy who do not deserve to be in a ditch along a country road, condemned to eternal oblivion.

At that time, while we had an abundance of work on our plates, we obtained a fundamental kind of help from two people who had come to meet us at the excavation site at Cubillos del Sil, Víctor Luis and Marisa, of the Cultural Society of Gijón. After relating to us the type of response our work in Asturias had had there, they offered to create the Asturian branch of our Association. In addition to freeing us from a portion of our work, this would allow them the ability to work in their own region with people with whom we were only able to have contact via telephone or mail.

However, our obligations to the UN had to pass a test of fire. On August 20, at 4:00 p.m. local time, the lawyer Montserrat Sans, granddaughter of exiled *republicanos* in France, entered the headquarters of the UN in New York, accompanied by three American International Brigade members. A few days prior, the members of the Lincoln Brigade had given us a list of 350 American citizens who had "disappeared" in the Spanish Civil War. Our intention was to try to internationalize the problem to put more pressure on the UN.

The Working Group on Enforced Disappearance has three meetings a year, two in Geneva and one in New York. That year, the meeting in New York was held from August 19-24, at which time its members met with different groups from around the world who were requesting help finding the "disappeared." Montserrat Sans prepared a brief text to outline the Spanish case and then studied everything related to our 1977 Amnesty Law to be able to answer anything they might ask her. The text she read provided an analysis of the situation and made a series of important proposals (Addendum 1).

After Montserrat's speech, the debate that ensued between her and the members of the task force dealt with the statute of limitations. One member of the group maintained that it was complicated for them to have the authority to research cases of disappeared persons prior to October, 1945, which is when the UN was created. Montserrat's viewpoint was that to strengthen our argument, we needed to find more cases of disappearance after 1945 to prove that what happened in Spain was a method of political persecution by the Franco dictatorship in a continuous manner, not simply as "collateral damage" from the Civil War.

12

The Mass Graves in the House of Representatives (*Congreso de los Diputados*)

I SPENT THE FINAL days of August, 2002 in Bayubas de Abajo, a town in the province of Soria where the first exhumation known to us occurred in 1970. The phone rang all day every day. Family members and reporters were hoping to get information, and our cause was becoming internationally known. Numerous foreign correspondents were interested in the case of the Spanish *desaparecidos*. *Le Monde*, *The Guardian*, *The Independent*, the *BBC*, *The Economist*, among others, were producing extensive reports, which we could use as leverage to pressure the Spanish government into helping us.

In the month of September, the Socialist Party representative to the Congress from León, Amparo Valcárcel, announced to us that she would make a motion to the Constitutional Committee of the House to debate the issue of the Spanish *desaparecidos* in the Civil War. Her decision created a conflict for us in that we, too, were writing a motion to give to all the political parties that had representation in the government to respond to the families' needs as a unified effort rather than a partisan issue. Although the Socialist representative submitted her motion, we continued preparing our own. Our attorney, Elena Reviriego, sent us the document which we then sent to all the political parties in question (Appendix III).

From then on, our strategy consisted of close contact with the media, especially the foreign press, to garner support that would influence the positive outcome of our proposal to members of Congress. Soon after receiving our proposal, the *Izquierda Unida* (United Left) coalition registered it for discussion in the House. A few days later, Eusko Alkartasuna (a center-left Basque nationalist party) did the same thing.

On September 6, we carried out our first exhumation outside of the province of León, in Caleruega, a town in the province of Burgos; the local government had approved the exhumation of four residents who had been murdered and buried in a common grave in the nearby town of Espinosa de Cervera. We exhumed the bodies of Alipio del Cura Aragón, his son Víctor del Cura Manso, Agripino Peña Peña, and Silvestre Peña Pérez, who were killed by a group of Falangists on August 4, 1936.

In early October, the Association for the Recovery of Historical Memory of Gijón was inaugurated. Dozens of cases had already been documented in the central office of the Cultural Society of Gijón. For us, it was of extreme importance for two reasons: we were already expanding into different parts of the country and, due to the amount of information that was continuously being sent to us, we were over our limit in time and resources. That same month, branches of the Association were formed in Valladolid and Extremadura.

On the 26th of October, 2002, the Association for the Recovery of Historical Memory was officially inaugurated in Extremadura in an emotional ceremony, more so given the testimonials of the relatives of the *desaparecidos* from that region. A day earlier, we had visited the cemetery in Mérida, where there is an unmarked grave with approximately 3,500 bodies. During the event, in the Library of Extremadura in Badajoz, there was frequent reference to the concentration camp in Castuera, one of the most notorious of the 104 that existed around Spain. At the end of the ceremony, a man approached me, saying that his father and three brothers had died in that camp. Some weeks earlier, I had written a report about the concentration camps in Spain, and I had not managed to obtain a single response from anyone who had survived that camp in Castuera and who could talk about its conditions.

We held firm to the strategy of having the House of Representatives approve a resolution aimed at helping our cause, though there was still no date set for its discussion in the Constitutional Committee. Unknown was whether the Partido Popular, which was in power, would vote for it. Until then, some members of the PP had spoken publicly about it. In August, Rafael Hernando, head of communications for the Party, had indicated that he understood how the government of a democratic country would help families who had suffered so tremendously. But there were mixed messages. In an interview with the BBC, the House representative and father of the constitution Gabriel Cisneros denied the existence of *desaparecidos* in Spain and implied that those who were unaccounted for had simply been killed in the war.

When we learned the date for the debate in Congress over the *desaparecidos*, we were filled with optimism; they had chosen November 20—the anniversary of the death of the dictator, Francisco Franco. It seemed impossible that on such a symbolic occasion the PP could refuse to approve our resolution.

13
The House Condemns Francoism

A T THE END OF October, we had a meeting with numerous foreign correspondents in the *Círculo de Bellas Artes* (a cultural organization) of Madrid. Represented were newspapers such as *Le Monde*, *The Guardian*, *The New York Times*; magazines and journals such as *The Economist*, *L'Express* and *Proceso*; television stations such as the German ARD; and huge news conglomerates. Twenty-one correspondents in all attended the meeting during which for two hours we discussed the work of the Association and answered questions. They were very interested in the problem, particularly in how a society like ours could live in denial of its recent past, as if the Franco dictatorship had not happened.

That day I had lunch with a television correspondent from Norway, who later interviewed me at the base of a statue to Franco that is still on display on a main street in Madrid, near the neighborhood of Nuevos Ministerios (northern part of Madrid). This reporter had worked for several years in Brussels. We talked about the possibility of the Spanish government approving means to help the families in question. He said that if José María Aznar was hoping to have a role in the European Union, this could be a terrible stain on his record, since Brussels (the seat of the EU) was the center of the politically correct.

As a result of the late October meeting with the media, on November 11 *The New York Times* published a full-page report entitled, "Spaniards At Last Confront the Ghost of Franco."[15] Our attorney

---

15 Elaine Sciolino and Emma Daly, "Spaniards At Last Confront the Ghost of Franco, *New York Times*, Nov. 11, 2002.

Montserrat Sans called me, full of emotion, from Washington when she opened the newspaper and immediately saw that report. The report discussed the steps Spain was taking to come to terms with its history of Francoism, including historians' books, novels, etc. Within the text was the following paragraph which could not have elicited many smiles in Moncloa:[16]

> But the government has not embraced the new era of openness. Perhaps that is not surprising considering that Prime Minister José María Aznar's conservative Partido Popular grew partly from Francoist roots and veteran politicians with connections to the Franco era remain close to the government.

On November 15, we received an email from the UN Working Group on Enforced and Involuntary Disappearance, informing us of the decision that had been made in Geneva and New York about our case:

November 8, 2002

Dear Sir:
It is my honor to write to you on behalf of the Working Group on Enforced and Involuntary Disappearances, to inform you of the decision that has been taken by this group at its 68th session taking place now at the United Nations Office in Geneva from the 4th to the 13th of November, 2002.

During our meetings, the Working Group carefully examined the information about enforced or involuntary disappearances that would have occurred in Spain and which your Association provided us throughout the year. The Working Group has decided that, although the time frame for the disappearances themselves is not specified for consideration of special public procedures by our Group, we will only consider those cases which occurred sub-

16 Moncloa, a section of Madrid northwest of the center, home to many central government offices.

sequent to the establishment of the United Nations, i.e., after October 24, 1945.

After analyzing the variety of cases you have sent us, and given the specific expertise of our Group, we have decided to send to the Spanish Government the two cases whose summaries are attached to this email. We hereby express our hope that the authorities undertake a proper investigation of the two cases for the purpose of determining the fate and location of the people of whose disappearance we were informed.

The Working Group would like to underscore that in no way do we wish to minimize the importance of the cases which we have not approved. This decision was made to prevent the establishment of a precedent for other countries and situations that would cause an overflow of work for the already overburdened responsibilities and workload of the Group, which has an ever-diminishing pool of resources.

The Working Group would appreciate the Association's contacting the respective families regarding this decision, and relating to us as soon as possible thereafter any observation, comment, or request for further information from our Group about the investigation that the family members or your organization might wish to formulate.

Finally, I wish to inform you that the Working Group will hold its 69th session in the Headquarters of the United Nations in New York from April 21-24, 2003. Accordingly, the Working Group receives representatives from governments, non-governmental organizations, and individuals during the first three days of its sessions. If your Association is interested in scheduling a meeting with the Group, I ask that you contact the Office of the Secretary of the Group, Office of the High Commissioner for Human Rights in Geneva, to choose a day and time for your meeting.

Sincerely,

Diego García-Sayán, President
Working Group on Enforced and Involuntary Disappearances

The decision was at least partly positive because, in addition to denouncing the use of forced disappearance as a means of persecution during the Franco years, it demanded of the Spanish government information about two people whose files we had submitted.

November 20 finally arrived. On watching the two members of the Partido Popular who were on the Constitutional Committee raise their hands, along with all other members from different political parties, in support of a multifaceted request to support our work (Addendum IV), we were overjoyed. We knew how vital this was for all the families who had had the courage to ask for our help, as well as for those who still had not dared to do so. That gesture was also a sign that allowed many families who had been marginalized by the defeat of the elected government in the war to once again raise their heads.

The unanimous condemnation of Francoism in the House of Representatives was something that had never happened throughout the transition to democracy. This was a historic moment. The reasons why the Partido Popular had voted for the first time the way it did in this case had to do with Spanish society's access to information that was spreading quickly about the truth of Francoism. Books about victims of the repression, concentration camps, the enslavement of political prisoners and the existence of unmarked and mass graves had created optimal conditions for needs that had to be addressed. On other occasions, and due to the general lack of knowledge about that portion of our history, the Partido Popular refused to condemn Francoism; hundreds of thousands of Spaniards truly do not know the reality of the Franco years. But as more people were learning what it was that the PP would not condemn, the situation was becoming more complicated, and maintaining that position simply to appease its most conservative constituency could be a high price to pay.

Two days after the vote in the House, we called a press conference in Madrid to ask the government to designate, with the greatest urgency, means with which to help the families of the "disappeared"; some of the people in question were quite advanced in age, and they wanted to be able to die with the peace of mind of knowing that their fathers or brothers had had a decent burial. Even Isabel González and Asunción Álvarez came to Madrid. They briefly told their stories and affirmed that the greatest "flowers" they could take to their parents in the cemetery would be the bones of their brothers and sisters. Their words were so heart-rending that the majority of journalists at the event were moved to tears.

At the end of November, the magistrate of Villablino (León) told us that she was going to use DNA testing to identify the seven bodies that had been exhumed from the grave at Piedrafita de Babia. We had succeeded in setting a very useful precedent for other cases. The numerous groups in the Spanish provinces that work for the recovery of historical memory now have the aid of this tool. Since that moment, our labor consists of obtaining help from the Government so that all the exhumations requested by the families are performed. In December, the news magazine with the highest circulation in the Low Countries, *Elsevier,* published an interview with the President of the Spanish Government, José María Aznar:

Question: In Germany and Italy the conservative parties have been apologizing for years for the actions of their dictatorial regimes. Have you considered anything similar?

Answer: I have no reason to ask for forgiveness. The history of the Spanish transition to democracy is one of profound reconciliation, and that is the basis upon which we must continue working. We Spaniards have decided to look to the future, and that is very important. Everyone has their responsibilities.

Q: What about as a moral gesture?

A. We have just approved a resolution in the House of Representatives whereby all the victims of the Civil War and the Franco regime will be remembered. In general, this is the spirit in which we need to be moving.

Q. The Government is prepared to help the families who wish to recover the remains of their relatives located in mass graves?

A. All the families of victims of the Civil War that we can help recover, whether they be from one side or the other, of course, we will help them.

Q. But until now there have been no funds for this work?

A. We are willing to study the proposals that are submitted to that end.

January of 2003 marked two years since we received permission from the Department of the Interior to create the Association for the Recovery of Historical Memory, two years spent speaking to thousands of people, with many people dedicating a great amount of time to seeing this project through. No one could have told us, when we opened the grave of the Priaranza Thirteen, that in two years so much, and of such significance, was going to happen. Through some mixture of fate and desire, we have tended a wound that is starting to heal. We are unaware to what extent the consequences of our labors have gone, but we are convinced that what we have done and what we are doing is significant for Spanish society, for the political culture of a nation that still has in its collective unconscious numerous vestiges of Francoism. We have contributed to the seeking of justice for the men and women who constructed our first democracy. Their families deserve dignity and to stop living as if they were guilty. We owe a great debt of gratitude to those men and women who supported the weight of the transition and all those people who died for their belief in a more just society.

14
The Incomplete Transition

THE DEATH OF THE dictator Francisco Franco on November 20, 1975 opened for thousands of people the possibility of seeking and finding their "disappeared" family members from the Civil War and the postwar period. The recovery of democracy in Spain, which had been interrupted for nearly forty years, encouraged many of those people to lose their fear and dare for the first time ever to look for some clue as to the whereabouts of their loved ones whom they had never been able to mourn in a cemetery.

The relationship between the new democracy and the Franco regime was well known. There were sectors of society that were demanding justice, specifically that those in the highest offices of the regime should be held responsible for the systematic infringement of human rights from the beginning of the war to the end of the dictatorship. Other more moderate sectors proclaimed, in the name of reconciliation, a preference for closure so that the democratic process would not be hindered by a latent conflict in Spanish society which had arisen with General Franco's seizing of power from the legitimate, democratic government of the Second Republic.

The very term "transition to democracy" is linguistically deceptive in that it denotes a form of government being established for the first time, that it had not existed previously in Spain. However, in November, 1933, Spain held its first officially democratic elections in which men and women had been able to elect their representatives as part of an electorate based on universal suffrage.

Spanish history since Franco's death is not a smooth course. In 1976, by order of the Secretary of State at the time, Rodolfo Martín Villa, all of the garrisons of the Civil Guard were to hand over all of their files relating to the Civil War, the postwar period and the repression during the Franco years. Thousands of documents arrived in the hands of a "historic commission" whose principal objective was to construct the narrative of the Civil Guard that democracy could accept. Mountains of documents were destroyed between 1976 and 1978, among which was an abundance of information about people who were "disappeared" during and after the war, information that today would be fundamental for discovering the whereabouts of many people whose families never stopped searching for them.

Finally, the political process was by and large directed by the Francoist leaders who wanted to have a democratic nation, preserve their privileges, and offer no accounting to the populace. The Law of Amnesty of 1977 was the best instrument for the Francoist elites to smooth the path to democracy and maintain control of the political process. This Law, which was offered up to Spanish society as a means to free the *rojos* from prison, was, without any doubt, the social construction of impunity for those responsible for the dictatorship. The Law's first two articles are the best example of what occurred in that negotiation between the democratic and Francoist elements (Appendix V).

The Amnesty Law meant that in the core of Spanish society, the long-awaited dialogue would never occur, and the heirs of the Franco regime would have carte blanche to stay in public life and retain all the privileges they had been awarded by the dictatorship.

In 1977, when the first democratic elections after Franco's death were held, Spanish society gave interim control of the government to the Unión de Centro Democrático (a centrist party), thus displaying its fear that entrusting it to the hitherto disenfranchised progressives would overly annoy the reactionary elements. Fear has been one of the most prominent features that those in political power have used since Franco's death—a fear that has pervaded without any clear political will interested in eradicating it.

It was during the elections of 1979 when change actually began to surface. The arrival of leftist parties in local governments, including towns and cities, indicated a real transformation of the political process for many families, and in some places, they began to have exhumations. Towns in Navarra, Asturias, Extremadura and La Rioja saw a marked increase in the opening of unmarked graves that had survived the Francoist repression as secrets that everyone knew.

In 1979 and 1980 there were numerous exhumations, particularly in La Rioja. In the towns of Alfaro and Calahorra, dozens of bodies were recovered, and the families of those victims protested and demanded justice. In some cases, the protests were held in front of the homes of gunmen who had carried out the executions. Yelling, "Murderers! Murderers!" the relatives demanded that those who collaborated in the killings take responsibility for their actions.

Suddenly, something occurred that completely changed the course of our history. On February 23, 1981, Lt. Col. Antonio Tejero Molina attacked the House of Representatives.[17] Mentally, the families of the "disappeared" returned to the Civil War or its aftermath, and the exhumations stopped, at least publicly. This was one of the main results of the attempted coup d'état. Many people who had exhumed the remains of their lost loved ones, seeing this dire situation—the attempted coup—caused them to put their immediate or family concerns on the back burner, and even now many refuse to talk with us about their *desaparecidos*.

The memory of fear was activated in thousands of Spaniards, a fear that even today is easy to recognize, particularly in the smaller towns where the perpetrators of violence are free under democracy, and no one would even point them out on the street. When, in the summer of 2002 we held the international volunteer work group, one of the duties of the volunteers was to ask in the towns if people would speak with them about the Civil War. Many people paled on hearing the request, and others simply closed their doors. For people coming from another country, it was difficult to understand how in a nation that had been under democracy for 27 years, people would not dare to converse freely about something they had lived through.

---

17 This attempted coup d'état, which paralyzed Spain for eighteen hours, is widely known as the "23f" for the 23rd of February, 1981.

In 1982, with the victory of the Socialist Party, things did not change in that any discussion of the Civil War was considered taboo. Many foreign correspondents who wrote about the exhumations that we sponsored have asked us how we reconcile the many years of Felipe González as head of the Socialist-led government in Spain not having resolved this issue. Our answer is that we do not understand it.

In the first years of the socialist government, soon after the attempted coup in 1981, public exhumations might have been seen as a delicate matter. But by 1990, with the socialists' third absolute majority, in a country that was now a member of the European Union and of NATO, and which had seen between 1986 and 1989 unprecedented economic growth, the time was right to set the record straight. Recently, Felipe González has spoken publicly about an interview he had before becoming president, in the office of Adolfo Suárez, with General Gutiérrez Mellado. According to González, the general advised him that if he won the presidency, he should not broach the subject of the Civil War, as there remained "burning embers" (it was still a very touchy subject). One can understand that particular comment as good advice coming from the military figure with the best reputation in Spain after the attempted coup. But it is incomprehensible that for so many years that message would carry more weight than the will of so many thousands of people who could have been helped by the government and who had a right to that help. And it is even more incomprehensible, given that the high percentage of men and women who were in mass graves were members of the PSOE. How many thousands of people have died since then without ever having had the opportunity to discover their missing relatives?

The *republicano* families have shown themselves to be examples of generosity to Spanish society, examples that until now the highest institutions of the State have not acknowledged. When in the years of the transition they sacrificed their rights for the good of the political process, they were taking the same attitude their parents and grandparents had taken in their day in defense of democracy. But the political parties and the various heads of government have done almost nothing to recognize their efforts and to return to them the dignity that was stolen from them throughout nearly forty years of dictatorship.

One of the most dramatic cases that have been presented to us was that of Jesús Pueyo Maisterra, from the Aragonese town of Uncastillo; he lost seven family members who were executed in the war, among them his father. In one paragraph of his letter, he says, "This is very difficult. But for me, there is no room for forgetting. I am going to be 81 years old, and it seems like it all happened yesterday. Needless to say, I will continue demanding justice and recognition as a victim of Francoism and demanding that the political class legislate to this end, admitting the great historical error that was the Franco dictatorship." And he later added, "We have the right to know where the remains of our family members are. I know we have a lot of obstacles in our way, but I think the biggest one is fear, which is still latent. I saw proof of that two years ago (in 2000) in Uncastillo where no one wants to talk."

Jesús Pueyo included with his letter 130 photocopies of all the correspondence he had sent out since 1977 regarding his family. He had written to the PSOE, the King, Aznar, the National High Court, the UN and the European Court of Human Rights. In not one of these cases did he receive a satisfactory answer. No one had moved a finger to help him locate any of his seven family members.

When we began working on the opening of the common grave in Priaranza del Bierzo, it had been exactly twenty-five years since Franco's death, and yet we observed a marked resistance to our broaching that subject. Little by little we have been paving the way to having the "disappeared" from the Civil War and the postwar period make their way onto political agendas. Without much forethought, the work we were doing constituted an implicit critique of the transition. In the future, we must assess to what point forgetting that part of our history was necessary. Nevertheless, our work is not exclusively concerned with the opening of mass graves. We are starting to record testimonials from people who are older than eighty years of age who lived during those years. It is an urgent task because, clearly, time is against us. We have the duty to rescue those people from oblivion, to acknowledge their return, and to give them their place in our collective memory. To this end, we plan a Part II of this book to provide names and biographies of some of the men and women who for so many years were erased.

Epilogue

ALMOST TWO YEARS HAVE passed since the first edition of this book was published, of which this is a close cousin. Since then, the relationship between Spanish society and its recent past (the Civil War and Franco dictatorship) has improved to some degree. More people are participating in more events to dignify the memory of the men and women who established our first democracy.

Social participation in these events has multiplied. Dozens of collectives all over Spain have been organized to work on this matter. Thousands of grandchildren have been mobilized to determine their true roots, to unearth their family histories and to respect their grandparents in a way that many years of democracy never has.

This mobilization has been publicized widely. A few months ago, there was a television announcement for an audiovisual encyclopedia of the Civil War. A little boy was sitting with his grandfather in a big armchair watching a documentary on television. When it ended, the grandfather asked his grandson if he was going to go out and play with his friends that afternoon. The boy thought for a moment and then said, "I think I'd rather just stay here and talk with you," more interested in what his grandfather had lived through during that part of history.

Advertising, so sensitive to new social tendencies, had detected a social group of consumers of history, the children of those who formed the Second Republic. Film, too, had captured that new reality. The director Patricia Ferreira presented the film *So That You Don't Forget Me* in Berlin in 2005, which portrays the story of a 22-year old man whose grandfather, a man deeply affected by the Civil War, has a special understanding with him that goes far beyond their personal relationship and is expressed in his surprising and detailed recovery of his family memories.

What began as a social movement is beginning to crystallize as a cultural phenomenon in different spheres. This is one of the goals we have been working toward since the beginning—that the *republicanos* who disappeared during the Civil War and the Franco dictatorship would emerge in the present, albeit through different avenues.

Another objective we have fought for is the inclusion of new content in school textbooks. A study by the German university of Leipzig measured the amount of space dealing with the twentieth century in Spanish textbooks published between 1979 and 1999. Then they measured the amount of space in those same textbooks that dealt with the Second Republic, the Civil War, and the Franco dictatorship—44 years, which should have represented a substantial portion of the text. However, hundreds of thousands of young people who studied those texts saw between only 2% and 9% (depending on the publisher) of the material dealing with that period of our history. Thus, at the very beginning of the transition, we saw the handwriting on the wall: the funneling of our difficult history into the abyss rather than into the minds of our citizens.

This is one of the pieces of the scaffolding of the transition that eventually breaks down. During the academic year 2005-2006 students in Asturias who are taking Contemporary History discover in their textbooks the case of the unmarked grave in Valdediós, exhumed by the Association's branch in Asturias in July, 2003. In the grave were found the bodies of fourteen nurses and three orderlies who had been working in what was then a psychiatric hospital.

The inclusion of new content in textbooks should be a way to turn the "funneling into the abyss" upside down. It should allow Spanish society to rediscover its own history. Abandoning a purely military account of the events and including personal accounts of the repression, along with the names of those involved, should also constitute a marked change in our education. This could also lead to having the twentieth century in Spain become a course in itself.

In 2003 and 2004, the Association continued its work of searching for the "disappeared." But the response to this work in our society was due to three principal events.

On December 1, 2003, the House of Representatives paid tribute to the victims of the Franco regime. This was an event framed as a celebration of the twenty-fifth anniversary of the Constitution. For the first time since the end of the dictatorship, men and women who had suffered because of it could enter the headquarters of popular sovereignty as guests of honor.

The event was attended by all of the political parties with representation in parliament, except the Partido Popular. Representatives of that party, which was in power at the time, commented that the tribute "smelled of mothballs." Their attitude seemed illogical, given that they had voted to condemn the Franco regime in the resolution of November 20, 2002, which also recognized the dictatorship's victims.

Our Association was invited to participate in the tribute in the House, and we were allowed to bring ten family members of *desaparecidos*. In the Hall of Columns of the Congress building, we were represented by ten men and women, all of whom had *republicano* relatives who had "disappeared" during the war. It was very emotional to see them appear with dignity to receive a much-deserved recognition. Approximately thirty-five associations were represented there, and they all had a chance to express their feelings and desires. We selected Isabel González as our spokesperson, the 85-year-old woman who was searching for her brother in the grave in Piedrafita de Babia and who had spoken publicly at several of our ceremonies. Due to the solemnity of this event in the seat of our government, however, she was visibly overcome with emotion. Following is the text she read that day:

From the Association for the Recovery of Historical Memory, we wish to dedicate this tribute to all those men and women who still today, in many parts of Spain, are afraid to speak freely about what happened to them during the Civil War and the Franco dictatorship. Our hope is hereby expressed that events such as this will help them to lose that fear and to enjoy the freedom that should be the basis of a democracy.

We also want to dedicate this tribute to all those for whom it comes too late. Thousands of men and women have died in silence these past twenty-five years since the transition to democracy without having received any acknowledgement, in spite of what they suffered and how they fought for this democracy.

We do not want to forget the thousands of people who cannot be here today, as this tribute certainly is theirs.

Our Association was created to search for all the men and women who disappeared during the Civil War and the postwar era. We are victims of the Franco dictatorship's violence, but we have the added misfortune of still having our loved ones in ditches and other roadside graves. We want to rescue them from this obliteration and give them a decent burial. We therefore request that the government do its humanitarian duty by helping us in our search.

Though she had to pause several times to compose herself, Isabel managed to deliver her heartfelt speech, and at the close of the event all of those on the program were photographed together on the steps of the Congress building. It was a celebration clouded only by the absence of any representation of the political party in power at the time. This was a missed opportunity to normalize our history and to do justice to those deserving of it.

OUR TRIBUTE: "RECOVERING MEMORY"

We had been thinking for quite some time about the possibility of organizing a great affair in homage to the *republicanos*, and we knew there was a biological urgency if we were to do it, given their advanced age. Batting around the idea of hosting a concert as a tribute to the survivors of the Civil War, in February of 2004 we contacted the singer Pedro Guerra's *Contamíname* Foundation.[18] The problem, of course, was that we lacked contacts and resources.

The idea was well received by Belén Guerra, one of the officials of the Foundation, so we got to work. She contacted Carmen Peire, an executive with Evohé Productions, who could handle the technical

---

18   A non-profit created by singer and poet Pedro Guerra to encourage solidarity for the marginalized members of society.

aspects of the concert. At first, we thought we could set it up in a large pavilion in Madrid and charge a cover for the expenses. But later we contacted the government of the nearby town of Rivas-Vaciamadrid which immediately signed on for the project. Both the mayor, José Masa, and the head of the cabinet, Juan Manuel Llorca, offered funding from the local government to move the project along.

We had a vague idea of what we wanted the concert to look like. Pedro Guerra started calling singers, actors and writers. Gradually things fell into place, and we were ready for the concert/tribute called "Recovering Memory," which took place on June 25, 2004, in the soccer field of the Cerro del Telégrafo sports center. The three months of hard work paid off, and what happened that day was one of the most important events in the Association's history. Twenty-seven writers, singers and actors participated, gratis. Our primary job was to attract as many *republicanos* over eighty as possible from all corners of the nation.

The morning of the event, while the technicians were setting up the stage, we wondered how many people would come. Attendance was free, so we had no way of knowing what to expect, though we did have confirmation from 350 honorees. Our sister association in Andalucía, the Association of Historical Memory and Justice, was bringing a busload from Seville. Our Association had arranged for another bus from El Bierzo, where we had begun our work back in October of 2000.

During the days prior to the concert, we had been able to calculate perfectly the emotional importance of what we were organizing. One day, a young woman called us to say that her father would be coming to attend from his home in Zaragoza. The daughter could drive him to the concert, but he would need a place to stay. We phoned him to offer to reserve a room for him in a hotel. The man asked if he should send us money, but when we said that the hotel would be paid for by the government of Rivas, the man burst into tears. No one from any government had ever given him so much as a pat on the back as recompense for all the years he had sacrificed since his youth fighting for the democracy that we enjoy today.

The concert was to start at 9:00 p.m., and the first honored guests began arriving at 6:30. It was an uncomfortably warm day, and we tried to have them wait in the shade or under the tents that had been set up to shield them from the sun. The local government Youth Council, which had recruited 200 volunteers to welcome the special guests and all other attendees, did an admirable job that day.

As the minutes passed, the soccer field was filling to capacity, including 741 men and women over 80 years of age who identified as *republicanos*. Watching them arrive was impressive as, clearly moved, they received their credentials, then seemed to dismiss the heat as they prepared to enjoy an evening that had not long been on their calendars.

The journalist Carlos Elordi read a speech he had prepared, and then immediately Lluís Llach sat at the piano; just as he was about to begin singing *La estaca*,[19] he apologized for the tribute coming so late. "So very, very late," he emphasized. Among the artists who participated were Bebe, Rosa Regàs, Lluís Llach, Javier Álvarez, Benjamín Prado, Gran Wyoming, Ruper Ordorika, Alfons Cervera, Luis Pastor, Lourdes Guerra, Miguel Ríos, Luis García Montero, Pilar Bardem (who read an unpublished text by José Luis Sampedro), Luis Eduardo Aute, Juan Diego, Pedro Guerra, Víctor Manuel, Ana Belén, Almudena Grandes, Ángel González, Ismael Serrano, Juan Diego Botto, José Antonio Labordeta, Manuel Rivas, José Sacristán (who read a text written for the occasion by Eduardo Galeano), and Paco Ibáñez. Two members of the International Brigades, Theo Francos and Bob Doyle, also took the stage.

Seated facing the stage were hundreds of men and women who were experiencing for the first time in twenty-nine years of democracy this public recognition.

There were two things that were particularly magical that night. One was the song Pedro Guerra sang for the first time, *Huesos* ("Bones"). Following is the chorus:

---

19 "La estaca" (The Stake) is a song written during the Franco regime which denounces repression and calls for freedom and collective action to take down the regime.

Y habrá que contar,	And we will have to reveal,
desenterrar, emparejar.	unearth, identify,
Sacar el hueso	take the bones out
al aire puro de vivir.	into the pure air of life,
Pendiente abrazo,	awaiting a hug,
despedida, beso, flor;	a farewell, a kiss, a flower,
en el lugar preciso	in the exact place
de la cicatriz.	of the scar.

These words could not have resonated more with the work of our Association. While he was singing, two giant screens projected images from the photographs of Eloy Alonso, an Asturian photographer, grandson of an executed *republicano*, who had brought his camera to some of the exhumations. On those same two screens were projected more than seven hundred photographs of men and women, many of whom disappeared during the war or the postwar period.

The following day, some of those who had attended the event described to us how emotional it was to see the faces of their parents on the screens in front of so many people and in such a positive light. One of the most gratifying results for us was to see how many thousands of people in their twenties attended and were clearly impressed, thus representing an increase in the hope that this work on historical memory would continue.

Although anecdotes do not construct history, at times they define it. For me, there was an important detail which showed me that all of the effort of the preceding few years had not been in vain. In January of 2004, the Association for Historical Memory and Justice of Andalucía held a special event in Seville, with an initial speech by the writer Rosa Regàs on a Friday afternoon. When she finished speaking, a man wearing a *republicano* flag around his neck spoke next. The event ended on Sunday afternoon. That morning during a coffee break, a girl approached me saying she was the granddaughter of a *desaparecido* from Marchena. As we spoke, her mother, Antonia, joined us, and the daughter said that her mother had never spoken with anyone from their town about her father's disappearance. She added that on Friday, when the mother saw the man with the *republicano* flag around his neck, she panicked, squeezing her daughter's hand and asking to where she (the daughter) had brought her. This single reaction symbolizes in a powerful way the fear from which thousands of people still suffer when the Francoist past is referenced. Five months later, in June (2004), Antonia attended the tribute to the *republicanos* in Rivas, and on seeing her there we realized that she was coming to terms with the past.

Also noteworthy is the fact that we had arranged for abundant medical personnel to be on hand, given the advanced age of the honorees and the hot weather. At the end of the night, the doctors told us that they had treated exactly one person: a forty-nine-year-old man who was drunk.

AN INTERDEPARTMENTAL COMMISSION FOR THE VICTIMS

On July 9, 2004, the Council of Ministers met in León. There it was announced that the Government had approved the creation of an interdepartmental commission to make amends, both morally and judicially, for the victims of the Civil War and the Franco dictatorship.

At last, there was now an official response from the central government which at least indicated that they had the intention of taking responsibility for our country's past, a point of departure for the adoption of political measures. Although the PSOE had hardly done anything by way of redress in its earlier administrations with Felipe González at the helm, the arrival at government headquarters of the new President, José Luis Rodríguez Zapatero, the grandson of a *republicano* captain executed by Franco's troops, seemed to have changed things.

On March 14, 2004, when the Partido Popular lost the elections, we tried to discern how the change in government would affect our work. We were scrutinizing every detail that might hint at the intentions of the new administration. One of the first clues we had was Rodríguez Zapatero's inaugural speech, at the end of which he quotes a phrase from the testament of his grandfather who, as an officer loyal to the government of the *República*, was killed by firing squad in León at the beginning of the war. The phrase, which represented his final wishes, is: "An infinite yearning for peace, love of goodness, and social

improvement of the downtrodden." The experience of the previous socialist government concerning the recovery of historical memory and
acknowledging the surviving *republicanos* had been disappointing. But
the arrival of this new president, who had not been part of the "pact of
silence" during the transition, opened a whole set of new possibilities.

In December of 2004 we met with the interdepartmental commission at the President's office. The four members of the Association's
delegation included Santiago Macías, the archaeologist Ángel Fuentes,
Isabel González (who was searching for her brother) and me.

Santiago Macías handed out a considerable amount of documentation and explained to the members of the commission what we were
dealing with. Next, I described the work we had done thus far and
what we were asking of the commission. Ángel Fuentes gave a presentation with projected images explaining the exhumation and identification processes. And finally, Isabel González spoke about the many
years she had spent trying to recover the remains of her brother Eduardo, and how in the early 1940's she had made a petition to this end in
Geneva at the headquarters of the League of Nations. She finished by
asking the commission not to waste time, as, given her age, she could
not wait much longer for an outcome.

It is time for the Government to take political measures to address
our past. Thousands of people are waiting for this, and they have a
right to this aid in a democracy. When Lt. Col. Tejero Molina burst
into our House of Representatives (which was in session), pistol in
hand, shouting, "Don't anyone move!" the memory of the Civil War
and the Franco dictatorship was palpable. Now the time has come to
situate these events in their proper place in our history.

Madrid, March 2, 2005

Appendix I

Participation of politicians in the homage to the victims of Francoism which took place in the House of Representatives on December 1, 2003.

Rosa María Mateo

Welcome to this House where men and women who were elected democratically by the citizenry make decisions every day on the laws that guide our daily life and our coexistence. The majority of us knew a very different Spain from the Spain of today, a country that is reflected in a poem by Gil de Biedma from which I have selected a few verses, as follows:

Media España ocupaba España entera,	Half of Spain occupied all of Spain,
con la vulgaridad, con desprecio total	with crudeness and the full disdain
del que es capaz frente al vencido	of which it is capable in the face of the vanquished,
un intratable pueblo de cabreros.	an intolerant mob of goatherds.
Con la luz de atardecer, sobresaltada y triste,	With the evening light, startled and sad,
se salía a las calles de un invierno	one would go out into the wintery streets.
poblado de infelices gabardinas	full of woeful raincoats
a la deriva bajo el viento.	adrift in the wind.

You will remember those raincoats. Many of them had on one sleeve a black band to symbolize a recent period of grieving. Spain was at that time a country of mourning, of absence, of silence. All of us together made change possible, but unfortunately during these years of democracy the terrorism of ETA[20] has again dressed us in black, and just two days ago seven Spaniards died in the line of duty in Iraq. I would like to ask for a moment of silence for them.

[After a moment of silence, the honored guests begin to shout, "NO WAR!" after which Rosa María Mateo continues:]

Today, only five days before our Constitution's 25th anniversary, the government's political parties, with the exception of the Partido Popular, would like to honor all those who suffered reprisals during the dictatorship. You are their faces and their voices. I don't know if you remember the end of the José Luis Garci movie *Asignatura pendiente* (*Unresolved Matter*). There was a long list of dedications, and the very last one read, "To Miguel Hernández, who died without our knowing he ever existed." This is how I would like to end my brief introduction, remembering all those who suffered persecution in the fight for freedom, while we did not even know they existed.

The program will now continue with the participation from the spokespersons of the parliamentary groups which have organized and promoted this tribute. We are going in order from the smallest group to the largest. The first to speak was supposed to be Mr. Joan Puigcercós, from *Ezquerra Republicana de Catalunya* (*Republicano* Left of Catalonia), who supports this event but had to be excused. Next will be Mr. Joan Saura of *Iniciativa per Catalunya* (Catalan Socialist Green Party)

JOAN SAURA, Iniciativa per Catalunya

My dear friends, good morning. This is an exceedingly important event for me. I believe it is the most important political event to be celebrated in the 25 years since the Constitution, because you

---

20 ETA *(Euskadi Ta Askatasuna*, Basque Homeland and Liberty), the Basque separatists who used violence to achieve their aims.

[applause], because you more than anyone else know that democracy has not been handed to us but that we have worked for it and achieved it, and really *you* have achieved it. Therefore, in the name of *Iniciativa per Catalunya-Els Verds*, I wish to acknowledge sincerely and profoundly all those who have suffered reprisals from the Franco regime simply because they fought for freedom and democracy. In spite of there being those who did not want this tribute to take place, this event is taking place and it will take place and it also has a dual significance.

First, it is significant because it is just. This is an act of justice for everyone—for all the men and women who were mistreated, imprisoned, tortured, in many cases killed, for defending the freedom of the Spanish nation. It is also an act of justice towards all those who have given part of their life, in some cases their whole life, for the democratic freedoms in Spain. And the other dimension that I wish to mention is that this celebration today is an act of strengthening our democracy, because a true democratic culture must be closely linked to historical memory and a solid knowledge of history. Knowledge of history is a vaccine against any authoritarian or military virus that might try to develop in our Spanish State. With this in mind, it is essential that we foster an anti-fascist culture, as France and Germany are doing. In the European Union, in Europe, democracy means anti-fascism, and fighting against fascism is a sign of democratic identity [applause]. I would like to finish by saying "thank you very much," because without you this event would not have been possible. Without you, we would not be here today, nor would we be celebrating justice and hope for a much more democratic future for the Spanish nation. That is all, and thank you very much.

Rosa María Mateo

José Núñez, of the *Partido Andalucista* (Center-Left Party of Andalusia), also planned to be here but has had to be excused. Next, we will hear from Begoña Lasagabaster, of *Eusko Alkartasuna* (a center-left Basque nationalist party):

BEGOÑA LASAGABASTER, of Eusko Alkartasuna

> Dear Friends, good morning to you all. On behalf of Eusko Al-
> kartasuna, I wish to say to all of you—to those who have suffered
> repression and exile personally, to those of you who are represent-
> ing others and to the families of those who unfortunately cannot
> be here—I wish to express two sentiments: first, that of homage
> and appreciation. Appreciation for your generosity during these
> long 25 years, for having sacrificed your own interests and justly
> earned vindication in the name of coexistence, after so much suf-
> fering. The second sentiment is that of a need for justice—justice
> for which we must all work, and work hard; justice to obtain for
> you decent living conditions; to recover memory, history, the re-
> ality of what occurred, in short, to secure the moral, social, and
> economic appreciation which is owed to you and your families.
> We do not wish to reopen wounds, rather we want them to heal
> permanently. But for that to happen, they first need to be treated,
> and to treat them we first need to acknowledge all the pain you
> endured, and nothing must be forgotten, and especially not now.
> To quote a great man, a hero of civilization in the face of brutality
> and fascism, forced into exile, a hero also of Basque nationalism,
> "war is punishment." These are the words of Manuel de Irujo, who
> also said that only with words, dialogue, freedom and justice will
> we be able to exist and coexist, respecting the dignity of all. To all
> of you, and from the bottom of my heart [she says first in Basque
> and then in Spanish], *ezkarrekasco*, thank you very much.

ROSA MARÍA MATEO

> We will now hear from Mr. José Antonio Labordeta, of the *Chun-
> ta Aragonesista* (Democratic Eco-Socialist Party of Aragon).

JOSÉ ANTONIO LABORDETA, of the Chunta Aragonesista

> Today is a day of mourning and of hope. Hope is what you have
> brought here, and we must thank you for your strength in defend-
> ing and supporting freedom. Forests are cut down, destroyed;

fields are broken up, but the roots remain and eventually they grow again. You realized this miracle with your resistance. Liberty has returned, democracy is reborn, thanks to you. The other day during a press conference I mentioned a carving on a stone monument to the 1,079 people executed near Teruel, which read, "We will only have died if you forget us." We swear we will never forget you, and we thank you for being here with us. Thank you very much.

ROSA MARÍA MATEO

Mr. Francisco Rodríguez of the *Bloque Nacionalista Galego* (Galician Nationalist Bloc) will now speak.

FRANCISCO RODRÍGUEZ of the Bloque Nacionalista Galego

I hope you will allow me to evoke certain names that are familiar to me and that with Galician specificity notwithstanding could represent all of you, men and women, who are here today. I evoke the name of Castelao,[21] who died in exile, and thanks to whose teachings many of us Galicians were able to learn about our country. I evoke the name of Alexandre Bóveda, Secretary General of the *Partido Galleguista* (Galician Nationalist Party), a man of deep Catholic faith, who was savagely murdered in the province of Pontevedra and whose memory the institutions of Galicia will not honor. I evoke here, before you, my maternal and paternal grandfathers, one of whom was imprisoned for allowing Azaña to use his balcony to give a speech in the government building of Xerantes [*sic*], near El Ferrol. My paternal grandfather escaped to the hills of Fragas do Eume[22] and, probably after having been caught, murdered and thrown into one of those unmarked graves, of which there are a surprising number in Galicia, lies abandoned, out of sight. I evoke Radio Pirenaica, listened to by my whole family, terrified, intimidated, in silence, but also with great emotion. I

---

21   Alfonso Daniel Rodríguez Castelao, founder of the Galician Nationalist Party.

22   A natural woodland around the Eume River in Galicia.

evoke the workmen of El Ferrol who on March 10 (1972)[23] burst out into the street, risking their lives to bring democracy to the Spanish nation and making us keenly aware that we urgently needed to end the Franco regime. But all these evocations where there is intimidation, where there is silence, where there is censorship, where there is repression—I want you to know that we in the Bloque Nacionalista Galego do not believe we have overcome them. We are in a historic moment, both at a national and international level, where there is so much silence, repression, censorship and manipulation to fight against. And I want to make a profession of faith here today with all those in favor of democracy in Spain that we are going to do everything within our power to see that there is established in Spain the politics of a pluralistic State that respects political diversity. We want a government that allows for diversity of opinion on all fronts so that the Spanish State can truly be plurinational, a truly democratic State, a nation of social justice and a nation that maintains in the world, on an international level, positions that are admissible and not the terrible situation we have now with an occupying army against the most basic rights of the people to self govern.

Rosa María Mateo

Ms. Soledad Monzón of the *Coalición Canaria* (Canary Islands Progressive and Nationalist Coalition) now has the floor.

Ms. Soledad Monzón of the Coalición Canaria

Friends, welcome to this, your home. It is a great honor for me to represent my party, the Coalición Canaria, at this important tribute, and especially so laden with emotion. Today the only protagonists are you men and women who suffered and fought for democracy. This tribute today must fulfill a dual objective. It is an act of homage, of recognition of that struggle that was fraught with death, exile, abandonment and the loss of liberty. But this is also

---

23   Workers' rights protests in El Ferrol, which were illegal under Franco.

a demonstration of appreciation. The new generations that have been raised in a democratic state hardly realize what it means. For that reason, we must commit it to memory, and thereby an event such as this and other similar tributes hold so much significance. Thank you all, sincerely.

ROSA MARÍA MATEO

Mr. Iñaki Anasagasti of the *Partido Nacional Vasco* (Basque Nationalist Party) now has the floor.

MR. IÑAKI ANASAGASTI of the Partido Nacional Vasco

Thank you very much and good morning. Speaking to you is the son of an exiled *republicano* and Basque nationalist, representing a party that had ministers in the government of Largo Caballero and Negrín,[24] and it is a great honor to be here. You probably remember—I imagine that you would have read the trial of Besteiro[25] here in Madrid. When Besteiro was asked where all the gold from the Republic was, he said it was in the cemeteries, at the walls of the firing squads, and in exile. And here, too, is the gold from the Republic, right here in this room. [Long applause.] This event has been called a "mothball revival." Well, welcome to the *republicano* and democratic mothballs rather than the the other blue[26] and imposing mothballs [Long applause] because we are talking about a legitimate Government based on a legitimate Constitution, the one from 1931. And when the other day you saw that terrible scandal that the Secretary of State [*sic*] Gómez Angulo caused in Melbourne at the Davis Cup when they played the Himno de Riego, that man should have been sent someplace that rhymes with his last name [an inappropriate word that rhymes with the name Angulo]. And you know why: because the Himno de Riego refers to that General Riego who fought against the ab-

24 Francisco Largo Caballero, Socialist politician and prime minister from 1936-37. Juan Negrín was the Socialist prime minister from 1937-1939.
25 Julián Besteiro, Socialist politician and university professor.
26 Color associated with the Spanish nationalists.

solute monarchy, and it was the official hymn of the Republic for nine years. One should be able to expect a little common decency, and that is what is expected of our leaders, yet it was not exhibited on that occasion.

To conclude, on this occasion, as we commemorate 25 years of our Constitution, we must remember that other legitimate Constitution. And we must also remember that in the Valley of the Fallen[27] lies the one responsible for that terrible war. Can you imagine if Berlin had a monument in homage to Adolf Hitler at his grave? No, of course not. Nevertheless, here we are admitting many things, including the lack of respect for this event. Notice, the Partido Popular condemns ETA, but we must remember that ETA is a consequence of Francoism. We condemn ETA and we condemn Francoism. But the PP has not condemned the Spanish Civil War nor the uprising against the legitimate Government. I am going to finish with something you all are familiar with. You remember the military dispatch from the war on April 1, 1939. "Today, with the red army captured and disarmed, the nationalist troops have reached their ultimate military objectives. The war has ended. Signed, El Generalissimo Francisco Franco." Well, I am going to turn that around: "Today, with the blue army in hiding, yet armed, the democratic and *republicano* troops are defeating on moral grounds the far right of the PP; troops of dignity, democracy and *republicanismo* have occupied the seats in Congress. The ideological battle for democracy continues. Signed, The Supreme Sovereign People." Thank you very much.

ROSA MARÍA MATEO

Mr. Josep Sánchez i Llibre, of Convergència i Unió (Convergence and Union Party, a Catalan Nationalist and Centrist party) has the floor.

---

27 The Valley of the Fallen, a controversial monument north of Madrid that served as Franco's burial site from 1975-2019.

MR. JOSEP SÁNCHEZ I LLIBRE, of Convergència i Unió

Friends, I want the first words from the parliamentary group I represent, Convergència i Unió, to be congratulatory on this well-deserved homage that all the political forces of Congress are celebrating. At the same time, we lament the lack of sensitivity of the PP, as well as their lack of political savvy for not attending this much-deserved tribute to what you represent today in this hall. With this homage we are not trying to settle accounts with any individual, but purely and simply with history and the truth, as the main political victims of dictatorships and civil war are these, history and the truth, as demonstrated by our own dictatorship and war, from 1936-1975. But from Convergència i Unió we wish to acknowledge the enormous generosity you have shown to our Constitution, whose 25th anniversary we are celebrating this week. We also wish to acknowledge that you have been the most forgotten members of the Constitution. For that reason, our parliamentary group, together with the others, have deemed it urgent that you be recognized and honored and that all future celebrations of this type for the protection and support of victims and their families have this same platform. I would also like to contribute here the good will of thirteen Catalan associations which could not take part in this event, specifically the *Asociació de Desenterrats del Franquisme a Catalunya* (Association of the Disinterred in Catalonia from the Franco Regime) and the *Agrupació de Supervivients de la Guerra* (Civil War Survivors Group). And finally, friends, on a personal note: the person speaking to you is the son of a soldier who enlisted with the *Agrupación de Carabineros de Catalunya* (Catalan Guards), the famous *quinta del biberón* (recruits under the age of 17), to fight, just as you did at that time, and who today would be honored to be with you. Congratulations. This has been an honor.

ROSA MARÍA MATEO

Mr. Felipe Alcaraz of *Izquierda Unida* (United Left) has the floor.

Felipe Alcaraz of Izquierda Unida

Fundamentally, this tribute is a homage to the struggle for freedom, a homage from the heart of popular sovereignty, organized by representatives of political parties who have received 11,700,000 votes, and thus we are the majority of the popular vote. But not only is this a homage to the struggle for freedom and democracy; it is also a refutation of what has been said about its being a "mothball" and resentment-filled revival. It is also a refutation of the barrage of carefully disguised propaganda from the Aznar era that this democracy was Franco's legacy. It is not! Here is the proof: the democracy that we have, and that must be strengthened every day, is not an outgrowth of the dictatorship, but something else. It is something very different. Therefore, so that our democracy will not be complete, so that the quality of our democracy does not improve, they are trying to eradicate people's memory, which is the reason we are all gathered here today. Many of us have come out of serious discussions and come to a consensus. We were always told, "To forgive is inhumane. To forget is a huge mistake." At the end, and with a very heavy heart, from heated discussions beginning in the 1950's, we finally have reached a conclusion: we are going to forgive, but we are never going to forget. [Applause.]

If we are able to create democratic hegemony, and I believe we are, among all of us, from now until the next elections, we are going to have to teach the PP the real history of our nation. Reconciliation may become part of our history if the government would abandon the idea that the foundation of our democracy is a consequence of the legacy of Francisco Franco. Additionally, the PP would not be allowed to use public money to support entities that the majority of Spaniards do not favor. Or how about this idea: we could charge an entrance fee of two million pesetas to those who visit the Valley of the Fallen—in the spirit of Mr. Arenas[28] or our Francoist heritage; maybe that would help the cause for reconciliation [stated with sarcasm]. Those of us who are paying attention see

---

28 Javier Arenas, Conservative politician.

everything that is happening. We could capitulate and say that the dead from the Blue Division[29] who fought side by side with the Nazi-fascists and are being buried with dignity and with proper monuments in proper places is cause for reconciliation, while the 600 Spaniards who fought for the freedom of Europe and finally achieved it, left their lives on the battlefield of Stalingrad.[30] Reconciliation could also be imagined when we run into Mr. Fraga[31] on the street and don't greet him, and if he speaks first, we return the greeting. But what reconciliation *is not* is to criticize this special event today, to try to obliterate memory, to say that this is about a bunch of troublemakers running around stirring up the past and holding a grudge and that it reeks of mothballs. This is not the case. It is a serious affair of enormous importance. You people have lived long and struggled greatly. You are the reason that everything happened after the dictatorship. Your fight has been priceless and unforgettable. Thank you very much.

ROSA MARÍA MATEO

Mr. Jesús Caldera of the *Partido Socialista Obrero Español* (Spanish Socialist Workers' Party) has the floor.

JESÚS CALDERA of the Partido Socialista Obrero Español

Welcome to Congress. Welcome, everyone, to this heartfelt and emotional homage. I am honored to speak on behalf of the Spanish Socialist Workers' Party. I am also convinced that, in spite of the Partido Popular's refusing to attend, all of us here are representing the great majority of Spaniards. For example, in this hall today we have Mr. Armando Benito, who was a senator from the Central Democratic Union. I am certain that many centrists and

---

29 The Blue Division was a volunteer unit of Franco's soldiers attached to the German army on the Eastern Front.

30 Beevor, Antony (2006). The Battle for Spain. The Spanish Civil War, 1936-1939. London: Penguin Books. p. 419.

31 Manuel Fraga (1922-2012), head of Alianza Popular, the precursor to the Partido Popular, and a highly influential government official.

people on the democratic right also wish to honor you with this tribute, in spite of the PP not wishing to be here. Spanish society owes all of you a historic debt of gratitude, and I hope that today we can settle it. Our Constitution of 1978 has been the Constitution of harmony, of consensus. Because it overcame a convulsive historical period, our democracy must not set its pillars upon lack of remembrance. It must never do that. It is an obligation, first and foremost political, but also moral and ethical, that all Spaniards celebrate this honor and express this to you, who have given the best of yourselves for our freedoms. Representatives of domestic and foreign exile, people who sacrificed their most beautiful possession, their freedom, people who saw themselves deprived of the basic economic means to survive, people who gave their lives. We honor them all, hoping not to offend anyone, and by honoring them we are honoring Spanish democracy. At the same time, as Felipe Alcaraz said, in paying this tribute we are preventing the forgetting of our history, or more than forgetting, the reluctance to remember. One woman who had to leave Spain, a great writer, María Zambrano, who was later awarded the Premio Cervantes (Miguel de Cervantes Prize for Literature) in 1989, upon leaving Spain spoke these poignant and tragic words: "Spain is becoming the strangled soul of Europe." Years later when she was able to return to Spain to receive her award, she made a plea against forgetting: "I do not forget, I do not want to forget, although when all is said and done, forgetting is creative. But unwillingness to remember, never. Intentional amnesia erases everything. Never that!" Because of that, because we cannot lose our memory, we must celebrate this tribute, without offending anyone, and we simply regret that the majority party in Congress, the Partido Popular, is not here with us today. Perhaps its past weighs on it too heavily. But the past does not weigh too heavily on you, it does not weigh too heavily on you, but with your past and your present you have given all of us Spaniards a bright future in freedom. Thank you for all of this.

Appendix II

Royal Decree 1891/2004, 10 September, by which is created the Interdepartmental Commission for the Study of the Situation of the Victims of the Civil War and of Francoism.

TABLE OF CONTENTS:

According to the content of the motion approved by the House of Representatives on June 1, 2004, the Council of Ministers agreed on July 23 to form an interdepartmental commission charged with studying the situation of those who, as a consequence of their democratic commitment, suffered harsh repression during the Civil War and the Franco regime until the restoration of democratic freedoms. This commission is further charged with proposing measures, both legal and other, that are required to offer these individuals adequate acknowledgment and moral satisfaction.

The agreement entrusted the Vice-President of the Government and Minister of the Presidency with the preparation and submission to the Council of Ministers the appropriate legal instrument for the creation of the commission, which will consist of the departmental representatives indicated in said instrument.

By virtue thereof, and in accordance with the provisions of article 40 of Law 6 of April 14, 1997, regarding the Organization and Operation of the General Administration of the State, as proposed by the Vice-President of the Government and Minister of the Presidency, with the prior approval of the Minister of Public Administration and the previous deliberation of the Council of Ministers at their meeting of September 10, 2004, I affirm:

ARTICLE 1. FORMATION.

1. The Interdepartmental Commission is formed to study the situation of the victims of the Civil War and the Franco era, as an organ chartered by the provisions in Article 40.1 of Law 6 of April 14, 1997, of the Operation of the General Administration of the State.

2. The Commission will be overseen by the Ministry of the Presidency, via his Under Secretary.

ARTICLE 2. PURPOSE

The following tasks will be taken up by the Commission:

a. The general study of the rights held by the victims of the Civil War and those who suffered persecution and reprisals from the Franco regime. The preparation of a report about the status of this issue.

b. The preparation of a report about how to access public and private archives for the purpose of achieving the goals of the Commission.

c. The preparation for submission to the Government of a bill outlining measures to be taken in order to offer adequate recognition and moral satisfaction to the victims.

d. Anything else the Commission deems necessary to achieve its ends, within reason.

ARTICLE 3. COMPOSITION.

1. The following members comprise the Commission:

a. The Vice-President of the Government and Minister of the Presidency.

b. The Under Secretary of the Presidency, who will act as Vice-President.

c. The Attorney General of the State, Director of Judicial Services of the State.

d. The Secretary General for Public Administration.

e. The Director of the Department of Institutional Relations of the Cabinet of the President of the Government.

f. The Director General of Consular Issues and Assistance.

g. The General Technical Secretary of the Ministry of Defense.

h. Director General of Personnel Costs and Public Pensions.

i. General Technical Secretary of the Ministry of the Interior.

j. Director General of Relations with the Courts.

k. Director of the Center for Political and Constitutional Studies.

l. Director General of Books, Archives and Libraries.

2. The head office of the Commission will be staffed by an officer from the Under Secretary of the Presidency, ex-officio.

3. When he is advised of the matters to be considered, the President ex-officio will call meetings with other high-level officers of the General Administration of the State and of other offices, as well as with their press secretaries.

4. The Commission must ensure the inclusion and participation of the social associations and organizations of the people affected by or connected to the issue at hand.

ARTICLE 4. WORKING GROUPS.

The Commission will be able to create working groups under the coordination of one of its members.

ARTICLE 5. OPERATIONS.

1. The functioning of the Commission will comply with the norms contained in Chapter II, Title II of Law 30 of November 26, 1992, of the Legal Framework for Public Administration and Common Administrative Procedure.

2. The President will create the meeting calendar, the methodology for the work to be undertaken, and, in general, will decide on all aspects required for the efficient working of the Commission.

3. In cases of vacancy, absence or illness, and, in general, when there is just cause, the members of the Commission may have a previously designated representative from their Ministry substitute for them.

SOLE ADDITIONAL PROVISION: PERSONNEL AND EQUIPMENT

The Commission will work with the personnel and equipment assigned by the Ministry of the Presidency.

FINAL ADDITIONAL PROVISION: EFFECTIVE DATE.

This Royal Decree will be effective beginning on the day following its publication in the *Boletín Oficial del Estado* (*Official State Gazette*).

Signed in Madrid, September 10, 2004
Juan Carlos R. (King Juan Carlos)
First Vice-President of the Government and Minister of the Presidency, María Teresa Fernández de la Vega Sanz

Appendix III

The United Nations' Declaration of the Protection of All Persons Against Enforced Disappearance

Resolution 47/133 approved in the UN General Assembly on December 18, 1992

ARTICLE 1.

1. Any act of enforced disappearance constitutes an affront to human dignity. It is condemned as a denial of the objective of the Charter of the United Nations and as a clear, serious violation of human rights and basic freedoms stated in the Universal Declaration of Human Rights and reaffirmed and developed in other pertinent international documents.

2. Any act of enforced disappearance removes the victims from the protection of the Law and causes them and their families grave suffering. It constitutes a violation of the norms of international law that guarantee every human being, among other things, the right to recognition as persons before the Law, the right to freedom and safety, and the right not to be subjected to torture and other cruel, inhuman or degrading treatment or punishment. It also violates the right to life, or it puts it in grave danger.

ARTICLE 2.

1. No nation will commit, authorize or tolerate enforced disappearances.

2. Countries will act on a national and regional level, and in co-operation with the United Nations, to contribute through all means to prevent and eliminate enforced disappearances.

ARTICLE 3.

Nations will take legislative, executive, judicial and other effective measures to prevent or eradicate the acts of enforced disappearances in any and all territories under their jurisdiction.

ARTICLE 4.

1. Any act of enforced disappearance will be considered, in accordance with penal law, a crime worthy of appropriate penalty, given its extreme gravity.

2. National legislative bodies may establish mitigating circumstances for those who, having participated in acts of enforced disappearance, contribute to the recovery of the living victims or voluntarily provide information that helps solve cases of enforced disappearance.

ARTICLE 5.

In addition to applicable prison sentences, enforced disappearances must involve civil action against the perpetrators, as well as against the State or the authorities of the State who organized, consented to, or tolerated such disappearances, regardless of the international responsibility of that State, according to the principles of international law.

ARTICLE 6.

1. No order or instruction by any public authority, whether civil, military, or otherwise, can be invoked to justify an enforced disappearance. Anyone who receives such an order or instruction has the right and duty to disobey it.

2. Nations will ensure that any order or instruction given, authorized or encouraged regarding enforced disappearances shall be prohibited.

3. In recruiting the officials charged with ensuring the compliance of this law, paragraphs 1 and 2 of this article should be kept in mind.

Article 7.

No circumstance, whether it be the threat of war, state of war, internal political instability, or any other dire matter, can be invoked to justify enforced disappearances.

Article 8.

1. No State will expel, return or allow extradition of a person to another State when there is genuine concern that the individual runs a risk of being a victim of enforced disappearance.

2. To determine if such motives exist, the proper authorities will review all pertinent considerations of the nation in question, including systematic, serious, clear or massive human rights violations.

Article 9.

1. The right to speedy and effective lawful recourse as a means to determine the whereabouts of persons deprived of their freedom or their state of health, or to specify the authority that ordered the suspension of freedom or executed it, is necessary to prevent enforced disappearances in all circumstances, including those outlined in Article 7 above.

2. Within the framework of that lawful recourse, the appropriate national authorities shall have access to all places where people who have lost their freedom are held, including all places suspected of containing disappeared persons.

3. Also having access to those places are other proper authorities designated by the law of the nation or by any other international arm of justice of which the State is a part.

ARTICLE 10.

1. All persons deprived of their freedom must be held in officially recognized places of detention and, according to national law, arraigned without delay before a judicial authority following apprehension.

2. Accurate information about the detention of those persons and the place or places the arrest was made, including transfer sites, if any, must be made readily available to the members of their family, their attorney and other persons with a legitimate interest in knowing that information, except where clearly opposed by the detained individuals.

3. In all places of detention, there must be a current record of all persons held in the facility. In addition, the State will take measures to keep analogous centralized records. The information contained in those records shall be available to those mentioned in the preceding paragraph, as well as all judicial authorities, other proper and independent national authorities, and any other proper authority designated by the national legislature or by any international legal body of which the State is a member, who desires to know the place where a certain person is being held.

ARTICLE 11.

The release of all persons deprived of their freedom must occur according to established and lawful guidelines to ensure that their release has in fact occurred and that it has occurred in such conditions that their physical condition and ability to exercise their rights are safeguarded.

ARTICLE 12.

1. Nations will include in their national laws the norms that allow certain government officials who are eligible to make ar-

rests to decide the conditions under which these arrests are to be made, and to know the appropriate penalties that officials who refuse to provide information about an arrest will face.

2. Nations will ensure strict control, with a marked understanding of hierarchical responsibilities, over all those responsible for apprehensions, arrests, detentions, imprisonment without bail, transfers and incarcerations, as well as over other government officials who are authorized by law to use force and firearms.

ARTICLE 13.

1. Nations will ensure that anyone who has information or legitimate interest and claims that a person has been the subject of an enforced disappearance has the right to denounce the offense before a proper and independent national authority, which will immediately proceed to perform an exhaustive and impartial investigation. Whenever there is cause to believe that a person has been the object of enforced disappearance, the State, without delay, will turn the matter over to the appropriate authorities to begin an investigation, including when a formal complaint has not been made. That investigation cannot be limited or hampered in any way.

2. Nations will see that a proper authority has the ability and resources necessary to carry out the investigation, including the necessary ability to demand the appearance of witnesses and the submission of pertinent proof, as well as to prepare without delay to do on-site fact finding.

3. Arrangements will be made for all those involved in the case, including the plaintiff, attorney, witness, and those who carry out the investigation to be protected from any mistreatment, intimidation or reprisal.

4. The results of the investigation will be communicated to all interested parties, as requested, unless this would hinder an ongoing criminal case.

5. Arrangements will be made to guarantee that any harm, any act of intimidation or reprisal, as well as any interference with respect to the presentation of a complaint or during the process of investigation, will be duly punished.

6. An investigation must be able to be performed according to the provisions outlined in the preceding paragraphs, as long as the fate of the victim of enforced disappearance has not been discovered.

ARTICLE 14.

When the conclusions of an official investigation warrant it, and unless they have been extradited to another country with jurisdiction conforming to the international agreement in effect in this matter, the alleged perpetrators of acts of enforced disappearance in a nation shall be turned over to the proper civil authorities for trial. Nations must take appropriate legal measures at their disposal so that any alleged perpetrator of an act of enforced disappearance under their jurisdiction or control should face trial.

ARTICLE 15.

The fact that there may be serious reasons to believe that a person has participated in acts of an extremely grave nature such as those mentioned in paragraph 1 of Article 4 above, whatever the motive, should be considered by the proper authorities of a nation as they decide to grant or refuse asylum.

ARTICLE 16.

1. The alleged authors of any of the acts mentioned in paragraph 1 of Article 4 above will be suspended from all official functions during the investigation mentioned in Article 13 above.

2. Those individuals may be judged only by proper jurisdictions of common law, in each nation, with the exclusion of all other special jurisdictions, in particular the military.

3. There will be no granting of privileges, immunities or special dispensations in these trials, notwithstanding the provisions specified in the Vienna Convention on Diplomatic Relations.

4. The alleged perpetrators of these acts will be guaranteed fair treatment in accordance with the Universal Declaration of Human Rights and other current international protections throughout all stages of the investigation, as well as during the trial and sentencing phases, if applicable.

ARTICLE 17.

1. All acts of enforced disappearance shall be considered permanent crimes as long as the perpetrators refuse to reveal the fate and whereabouts of the disappeared person and as long as the case is unsolved.

2. When the resources provided in Article 2 of the International Agreement on Civil and Political Rights are no longer effective, the statute of limitations relative to the acts of enforced disappearance shall be suspended until those resources are re-established.

3. With regard to a statute of limitations, in cases of enforced disappearance, this should be lengthy and commensurate with the gravity of the crime.

ARTICLE 18.

1. The perpetrators or alleged perpetrators of acts outlined in paragraph 1 of Article 4 above shall not benefit from any special Law of Amnesty or other analogous measures that could exonerate them from any criminal proceeding or sanction.

2. When the right to grant a pardon is under consideration, the extreme gravity of acts of enforced disappearance should be duly considered.

ARTICLE 19.

The victims of acts of enforced disappearance and their families should receive reparations and will have the right to be compensated in an appropriate manner, as well as have access to means that would ensure as complete a readjustment as possible. In the case of death of the victim due to their enforced disappearance, their family will have the same right to compensation.

ARTICLE 20.

1. Nations will prevent and suppress the appropriation of children from parents who are victims of enforced disappearance or of children born during the captivity of their mothers who were victims of enforced disappearance, and they will make the effort to find and identify those children and return them to their original families.

2. Given the need to act in the best interests of the children mentioned in the preceding paragraph, it should be possible in nations that have a system of adoption to examine the adoption process of the children in question and, in particular, to nullify any adoption that originated from an enforced disappearance. Nevertheless, such an adoption may be declared legal if the child's closest relatives give their consent on examining the validity of the adoption.

3. The appropriation of children from parents who are victims of enforced disappearance or of children born during the captivity of their mothers who were victims of enforced disappearance, as well as the falsification or suppression of documents that attest to their true identity, constitute crimes of an extremely grave nature which should be punished accordingly.

4. To that end, nations will create bilateral or multilateral agreements.

ARTICLE 21.

The provisions of the present Declaration are without prejudice to those outlined in the Universal Declaration of Human Rights or any other international charter and should not be interpreted as a restriction or abrogation of those provisions.

Appendix IV

Text presented by Montserrat Sanz to the Working Group of the
United Nations on Enforced and Permanent Disappearance
(New York, August 2002).

On the 28th of October 2000, a group of archaeologists began
working on the exhumation of an unmarked grave in which were
found the remains of thirteen *republicano* civilians who were murdered by gunmen of the Falange. The family of one of the victims
had prompted the exhumation. Over the course of the days in
which the archaeological excavation was being performed, many
people from neighboring towns approached the site to say that
they, too, had parents, siblings or grandparents who had "disappeared." Thus arose the "need" to create the Association for the
Recovery of Historical Memory.

In Spain there are more than 30,000 people in unmarked graves,
deprived of their rights to maintain their identity after death, to
have their remains in a decent burial place where their families
can remember them in peace and mourn their loss. Some common
graves are immense: in Mérida, 3500 people; in Oviedo, 1600; in
Gijón, 2000; in Seville, 2500; in Teruel, 1005, etc.

During the 1970's in Spain, after the death of the dictator Francisco Franco, in towns all over the map, exhumations from common graves were performed. Family members had waited until the
end of the dictatorship to learn about their deceased relatives and
to exercise their right to give them a decent burial. In some areas,
families had demonstrated outside the homes of the killers. But

on February 23, 1981, there was an attempted coup d'état. Antonio Tejero Molina, a Lieutenant Colonel in the Civil Guard, burst into the House of Representatives and for almost twenty hours held the recently recovered Spanish democracy hostage.

Among the myriad effects of this attempted coup was the terror it inspired in the families who were opening common graves to locate their missing relatives, as they subsequently refrained from doing so. Many of the people who exhumed bodies then are now suddenly unwilling to speak about it, as the attempted coup caused them to think that there could be another civil war or another harsh repression similar to the one unleashed by Franco. It should be remembered that Franco, on October 1, 1937 displayed in his legislative bulletin two medals with the red arrows in the shape of a cross for Adolf Hitler and Benito Mussolini.

Until that 28th day of October 2000, when the grave containing the remains of the Priaranza Thirteen was opened, there had been sporadic exhumations, but none involving a group of anthropologists and medical examiners. This past March 16th, Professor José Antonio Lorente of the Department of Medicine at the University of Granada, a consultant for several Latin American governments on the identification of "disappeared" persons, took samples of four bodies for DNA testing. The results will be available in the middle of next September, and they will be the first victims of the Civil War to be identified through this type of testing.

One of the main difficulties with which the ARMH has to contend in its work is fear. In many towns in Spain, people are still afraid to talk about the Civil War and the years of the Second Republic during which, on November 19, 1933, true democracy was ushered into the nation with universal suffrage, with men and women electing for the first time their political representatives. The Spanish transition to democracy [1976-78], which was actually a recovery of democracy, was brought about by leaving along the side of the road the responsibility that any democracy has to the victims of a dictatorship. But now, years later, as happened with France and Germany due to their relations with Nazism, it seems that the time has come for us to assume that responsibility in a mature and calm way, without its causing any political turmoil.

This is humanitarian work, to allow the victims to recover the dignity that they lost during the dictatorship and which after twenty-seven years of democracy, they still have not recovered. The injured parties include political prisoners who built important public works and contributed to multiplying the assets of major construction firms; the thousands of Spaniards who were deported to Nazi concentration camps with the collaboration of the Francoist government; the political prisoners who remained incarcerated for years, etc.

What the Association for the Recovery of Historical Memory requests of the Working Group on Enforced and Permanent Disappearance is that it apply resolution 33/147 of December 18, 1992, whose text as a convention is now being edited, and which was ratified by the Spanish Government. For that resolution to be put into effect, the following steps must be taken:

The Spanish Government must finance the exhumation of the bodies and identification of the persons found in the unmarked graves if the families so desire. Other families will be satisfied with the placement of a gravestone or marker as a reminder of those men and women who built and defended the first Spanish democracy. In that sense it is imperative to work with haste, as the people who remain of the generation that lived the war are very advanced in age, and the day they disappear we will also lose the basic information on the location of the common graves, most of which have not been marked out of fear.

The military archives must be opened, as they contain thousands of files on people who were executed and which still, sixty-three years after the end of the war, remain restricted under military jurisdiction. With regard to this, we request that all files related to the Civil War be digitized so that people may visit their respective local governments and request a printed copy of a file on a family member. In many cases, the military archives contain personal objects that belonged to those executed, including letters written to their families on the day prior to their execution, and we believe the families have the right to those objects of a personal nature.

The dignity and defense of the victims is predicated upon the removal from all cities and towns of Spain the numerous monuments that still extol the dictator Francisco Franco and many of the leaders of his regime. We believe the families of the victims have the right to enjoy a dignity they currently do not have while we still have plaques and statues claiming that the Francoist military that ordered the execution of dozens of civilians were the "liberators" of cities and towns.

The Government should host a singular tribute to all the people who defended democracy against Franco, and which will serve as a symbolic act so that all the victims of the repression can recover political confidence and lose their fear of talking about the most tragic thing that occurred in their lives.

We hope that this Working Group helps in the recovery of the dignity of millions of people who are personally affected by the Francoist repression and the consequences of a dictatorship which lasted thirty-nine years and which, according to recent studies, at the end of the war, had murdered approximately 50,000 people. [32]

---

32 Julián Casanova, et. al. *Morir, Matar, Sobrevivir: La violencia en la dictadura de Franco*. Ediciones Crítica, 2002.

Appendix V

Motion Presented by the Association for the Recovery of Historical
Memory to All Spanish Political Parties

In Spain there are more than 30,000 unidentified bodies lying in mass
graves, among which is that of the internationally famous poet Federico García Lorca. Some of these graves, such as those in Mérida, contain some 4,000 bodies, and in Oviedo, 1,600; in León, 1,000 bodies;
Madrid, 1,000, and Badajoz 3,000. However, during and after the Civil
War, the Francoist government allowed its supporters who had lost a
family member to the *republicano* cause to exhume the body and take
it to the family home, and then, subsequently, the following orders
were handed down:

> Given the high number of legitimate requests to move the bodies
> of those killed in battle from one place to another of the territory
> occupied by our Glorious Army [the nationalist army], requests
> that are generally granted . . . since the current circumstances re-
> quire making these transfers of those who gave their life for the
> Fatherland as easy as possible . . . , I [Francisco Franco?] make the
> following concessions:
>
> 1. That through the proper authorities, once the transfer has been
>   authorized by the Military Authority, the best possible con-
>   ditions should prevail, in conjunction with health consider-
>   ations, for these transfers, which should be overseen by offi-
>   cers of this General Government [military government] . . . ,
>   destined for the transfer of bodies of those killed in battle or

as a result of wounds or illnesses linked to the same, and they [families] should be offered the lowest possible fee (Ministerial Order of October 22, 1936).

By Order of the 6th of May 1939, anyone who wished to exhume the body of a relative killed by the Marxist horde in order to be interred in a cemetery could request it without having to pay for a health inspection of any kind.

> . . . This Department offers assistance to the families of those who gloriously fell victim to the red barbarity for God and for Spain, to wit:
>
> 1. Any person who desires to exhume the body of a relative who was killed by the red horde, in order to bury it in a cemetery, may request it of the civil governor of the corresponding province.
>
> . . . .
>
> 4. The orders of October 22, 1936, and October 31, 1938 are in effect, as long as they do not conflict with the present order of May 1, 1940.

Orders were also handed down on February 7 and July 22, 1940, and yet the families of the losing side were not permitted to give a decent burial to their war dead; rather, they were left tossed into mass graves. As of this writing, this practice has not been abolished, contravening Article 14 of the Spanish Constitution of 1978, the right to equality, and violating both directly and indirectly international agreements in effect at this time.

The Geneva Convention of July 27, 1929, on the Treatment of Prisoners of War, which was signed by the Spanish Government on August 6, 1930, included provisions for "those wounded and infirmed on the battlefield," stating that:

> The warring factions will advise each other in the briefest possible time frame of the names of the wounded, sick or dead who are

retrieved or found, as well as all manner of identifying them. They will prepare and transmit the death certificates.

All objects of personal use found on the battlefields and on the dead will also be handed over, especially their dog tags, half of which should be left on the body.

Measures should be taken to ensure that the burials or cremations of the dead are preceded by a careful examination, preferably medical, of the bodies to verify death, establish identity and be able to prove both.

The bodies should be buried honorably, and their tombs respected and always able to be located.

. . . . At the conclusion of the hostilities, lists of the tombs and of the buried dead shall be exchanged with the opposing side (Article 4).

The Agreement of August 6, 1930, regarding Treatment of Prisoners of War, signed by the Spanish Government.

In the great majority of the mass graves are bodies of Spaniards "disappeared" after their arrest by armed groups allied with General Franco. In some cases they "disappeared" at the hands of government officials months after the end of the war and with the Franco regime firmly in place. All of them were suspected of having fought for the *republicano* government or being allied with same. None of them were treated equitably, neither by the courts nor by any other institution of the nation, which has impeded the discovery of the circumstances surrounding their deaths, as well as the ability to locate their bodies and allow their families to give them a decent burial.

During the 1970's in Spain, after the death of the dictator, some spontaneous exhumations were carried out by families of victims. Nevertheless, this process ended with the attempted coup on February 23, 1981, by Lt. Col. Antonio Tejero Molina and the belief that the recent Spanish democracy would not be able to reconcile with its past. The collective effect was that one sector of the population, already harshly beaten down by the repression of the Franco regime, was dissuaded from resuming or initiating the exhumations, once again suspending their repressed grief.

Finally on October 28, 2000, some family members decided to open the grave of the thirteen *republicanos* in Priaranza del Bierzo, with the altruistic collaboration of a group of anthropologists and medical examiners, and prompted by the Association for the Recovery of Historical Memory.

On March 16, 2002, the University of Granada, given the archaeological nature of the excavation, authorized an expert to take samples of four of the bodies exhumed. Those results will be ready in mid-September, and they will be the first non-combatant victims of the Civil War to be identified in this way. In contrast, and to illustrate the discriminatory treatment of the victims, the Spanish Government recently released millions of pesetas to exhume and repatriate from Russia the bodies of several Spanish volunteers of the Blue Division, a military group offered by Franco as a sign of friendship to Adolf Hitler to support the Nazi troops during World War II.

Another example worthy of mention is the cemetery next to the monastery of Yuste in Extremadura in which the Germans who were killed in Spanish territory during the first and second world wars were given honorable burials, and where each of the tombs identifies the soldier with a plaque of tribute to those brave foreign combatants.

Due to these circumstances, the Association for the Recovery of Historical Memory has received an exorbitant number of requests to continue its work in all areas of Spanish territory in order to establish the truth regarding events, and to exercise the right to give all victims a dignified burial. For the record, this petition was presented to the United Nations on August 5, 2002.

The conflict of the two Spains has not ended, nor will it end until the historical truth comes to light and the pain endured by so many families is recognized through the act of returning to them the bodies of their relatives so they may have a decent grave.

Those who lost the war were condemned to an imposed silence by the dictatorship and an agreed upon silence by the democracy after the Law of Amnesty of 1977 [see Addendum VII], a sentence that even now affects the third generation of the families in question. Perhaps we are hoping that this will also affect the fourth generation? [rhetorically asked].

The voices of all these people were relegated to a long and sad silence. Even today, there are those who lower their voice when they speak about the tragic past and even close their windows as if the topic were taboo.

For all these reasons, we request:

1. That the Spanish government, through its public institutions, comply with the duty to investigate and report the facts, ordering the exhumation of the bodies which are in mass graves since July 1936.

2. That the Spanish government begin the process of identifying the bodies and officially returning them to their families, taking every measure possible to facilitate this process so that they can be interred in the cemeteries of the families' choosing, just as was done with those of the *nacionales* [the Francoist forces].

3. That by means of plaques in their honor and all other corresponding manner of tribute, the dead may be recognized as people who once fought in defense of a legally elected government, in spite of having lost the war.

4. That all historians and family members of the victims who wish to know what happened to their relatives be reminded of their right to access Civil War archives.

5. That the Spanish government make available the means for reparation and dignification of the memory of the victims and put an end to the discrimination and lack of equal treatment of their relatives.

Appendix VI

Text Agreed Upon by the Spanish Political Parties, and Approved
by the Constitutional Commission on November 20, 2002.

To the Executive Committee of the House of Representatives:

The undersigned parliamentary groups present the following trans-
actional amendment to the motion proposed by the Parliamentary Group of the United Left regarding the recognition of the
moral stance of all the men and women who suffered repression
under the Franco regime for defending freedom and democratic
convictions; from the Socialist Group which urges the Public Administration to morally redress the situation of the victims of the
Civil War who were "disappeared" and murdered for defending
republicano values, as well as to acknowledge the right of families
and heirs to recover their remains, their name and their dignity;
from the Socialist Group regarding the development of a government policy to acknowledge exiled citizens; from the Federal Parliamentary Group of the United Left, in favor of the exhumations
of mass graves from the Civil War.

Madrid, November 19, 2002

Modified Amendment

The text will be edited in the following manner:

The Constitution of 1978, known widely and accurately as the
Constitution of Harmony, intended to put an end to the tragic
past of civil confrontation among Spaniards. Civil wars, military

rebellions, dictatorships, political regimes or systems based on the violent imposition of ideologies or forms of government had been until then the tragic reality suffered by the great majority of Spaniards, as if our fate were that of a collective failure. That sad lament by the poet Antonio Machado, "Little Spaniard who comes into the world, may God protect you. One of the two Spains is bound to freeze your heart," is a realistic reflection of this dramatic existential reality of the Spanish nation.

Fortunately, however, in 1978, a generation of Spaniards, recalling the lament of that other great Spaniard, Manuel Azaña—when he was overcome by the magnitude of the civil tragedy and spoke those dramatic words that sadly fell into nothingness, "Peace, mercy, forgiveness,"—decided never to commit the old mistakes, but to look ahead and, with a generous impulse of reconciliation, to bet on a new democratic system of government so that never again would there be two Spains inevitably at each other's throat.

The spokespersons of the main political groups left this spirit of national harmony at the Constitutional Convention, and it is well worth remembering at this juncture.

The current Spanish Constitution is steeped in that desire for coexistence. All of the constituents, for the sake of that basic consensus geared toward the establishment of a lasting democratic framework, made important concessions, including long-held, critical positions, to look for common ground capable of overcoming old, recurring conflicts.

And so, it was only months after the first democratic elections, with the approval of amnesty on the table, when this will to coexist in forgiveness and to leave the past behind became manifest. From among many eyewitness accounts, we single out the following:

"For us, as much as for reparations for injustices committed throughout these forty years of dictatorship, amnesty is a national and democratic policy, the only tool that can close that history of civil wars and crusades. We want to open the way to peace and liberty. We want to close one chapter and open another one. We, specifically, the communists, who have so many wounds, who have suffered so much, have buried our dead and our resentment. We are resolved to march ahead on that road to freedom, on that road to peace and progress.

(Rep. Camacho Abad, Spokesperson for the Communist Group)

"Amnesty is the fruit of the will to bury a sad time in Spain's history and to build another one upon different assumptions, overcoming the division that the Spanish people have suffered these last forty years."

(Rep. Benegas, Spokesperson for the PSOE)

Amnesty is simply a decision to forget, . . . an amnesty for all, everyone forgetting for the sake of everyone. . . . . This is not the time to allege acts of bloodshed, as there have been acts of bloodshed on both sides, some for power, some terribly sad and others terribly treacherous. . . . . Amnesty is a path to reconciliation but also to credibility and to a change in behavior."

(Rep. Arias Salgado, Spokesperson for the UCD)

The almost unanimous vote of Parliament in favor of the Law of Amnesty of 1977 was a historic event since it put an end to the confrontation of the two Spains, forever buried then and there. It is true that some refused to join that spirit of reconciliation and tried everything in their power to prevent, by means of violence or terror, the will of national harmony rooted in the fruits of peace and freedom for all. They have not prevailed, nor shall they ever.

This year marks the twenty-fifth anniversary of the return to democratic freedoms, and next year we could commemorate the first quarter century of the Constitution of 1978. Sixty-six years have passed since the beginning of the Civil War of 1936, and hardly any survivors of that terrible tragedy remain. Nothing, of course, remains in Spanish society of the civil conflict, because consciously and deliberately, it was decided that we must turn the page so as to avoid old resentments, avoid rekindling old hatreds, avoid fanning the flames of revenge.

On the other hand, in these last twenty-eight years there have been numerous provisions made by the central government and also by the autonomous communities that address, to the extent possible, reparations to the dignity of persons who suffered persecution during the Franco regime and to give them the necessary resources.

Within this group of people who suffered the tremendous consequences of war are the exiles. In September of 1999, Congress approved a motion regarding the commemoration of the sixtieth anniversary of Spanish exile since the end of the Civil War. To this end, the Pablo Iglesias Foundation[33] has prepared the exposition "The Indisputable Contribution of the Exiles to the Recovery of Freedoms in Spain," a contribution that allowed us to face the political changes taking place during the transition to Spanish democracy.

Diasporic exiles lost everything, and they have never overcome the pain of the exodus, because the forced departure from one's homeland is one of the most painful events imaginable. The idea of reconciliation is irrelevant to this group of people, many of whom, when they could return to Spain did not, since over the course of sixty years they made new lives in the countries that took them in.

Due to their firm convictions and the suffering they endured because of a war unbecoming a nation whose reason for being is to respect democratic values, the House of Representatives considers it a duty to offer a tribute of admiration and affection to those exiled citizens, as well as the so-called "children of war," who have survived that tragic episode of our history.

Given all of the above:

First, the House of Representatives, on this twenty-fifth anniversary of the first free elections of our current democracy, reiterates

---

33   Pablo Iglesias, a Marxist, was the father of Spanish socialism.

that no one may feel legally entitled, as has happened in the past, to use violence to impose their political convictions on others or to establish totalitarian regimes against the freedom and dignity of all citizens, actions that deserve condemnation and repulsion from our democratic society.

Second, the House of Representatives reiterates that the best course of action for our democratic coexistence is to uphold the spirit of harmony and reconciliation that presided over the writing of the Constitution of 1978, and which eased the transition from dictatorship to democracy.

Third, the House of Representatives reaffirms once again the duty of our democratic society to recognize the moral value of all the men and women who were victims of the Spanish Civil War, as well as all those who suffered repression under the Franco dictatorship. We urge any initiative prompted by the families of those affected to be undertaken, particularly in the local sphere, and that they receive support from government institutions, without reopening old wounds or stirring the embers of the civil confrontation.

Fourth, the House of Representatives urges the Government to quickly develop a complete policy of recognition and protective, economic and social action for those Civil War exiles, as well as for the "children of the war," including recovery of Spanish nationality for them and their direct descendants, as well as the right to vote.

Appendix VII

The Law of Amnesty of 1977 (First Two Articles)

ARTICLE ONE

1. The following are hereby granted amnesty:

a. All crimes and offenses of a political nature, regardless of the result, which were committed prior to December 15, 1976.

b. All acts of the same nature committed between December 15, 1976, and June 15, 1977, when the political motive was to restore general freedoms or regional freedoms to the people of Spain.

c. All acts referred to in the previous paragraph that occurred until October 6, 1977, provided there was no serious violence against the life or the integrity of those involved.

2. By the moment of the commission of the acts in the previous section, we mean the time in which the criminal activity was initiated.

Amnesty also includes crimes and offenses connected to the previous section.

ARTICLE TWO

All of the following are granted amnesty:

a. Crimes of rebellion and sedition, as well as crimes and offenses committed during these or because of these, described in the Code of Military Justice.

b. Conscientious objection to military service, for ethical or religious reasons.

c. Crimes of refusal to aid Justice by refusing to reveal facts of a political nature that are known in the exercise of one's profession.

d. Acts of expression of opinion in the press or any other media.

e. Crimes and offenses that could have been committed by the authorities, officials and agents of the public order, with motive or occasion of the investigation and persecution of the acts included in this Law.

f. Crimes committed by officials and agents of the public order in violation of the rights of persons.